Mom University
The Student Guide

by Danae Branson

PublishAmerica
Baltimore

© 2005 by Danae Branson.
All rights reserved. No part of this book may be reproduced, stored in a retrieval system or transmitted in any form or by any means without the prior written permission of the publishers, except by a reviewer who may quote brief passages in a review to be printed in a newspaper, magazine or journal.

First printing

ISBN: 1-4137-5449-X
PUBLISHED BY PUBLISHAMERICA, LLLP
www.publishamerica.com
Baltimore

Printed in the United States of America

To my two beautiful children -
you are my inspiration.

To my wonderful husband -
thank you for supporting me and my dreams.

You may have graduated high school, you may have graduated college, you may have even joined the military but nothing will prepare you for this!

Table of Contents:

9	Section 1	Introduction
13	Section 2	Students
15	Section 3	Academics
21	Section 4	Schedules
23	Section 5	Living
27	Section 6	Dining
29	Section 7	Transportation
31	Section 8	Childcare
33	Section 9	Health & Safety
37	Section 10	Finances
39	Section 11	Support Services
41	Section 12	Visitors/Prospective Students
44	Section 13	Orientation
46	Section 14	Books
48	Section 15	Colleges & Departments
65	Section 16	Hardcore Years
68	Section 17	Extracurricular Activities
69	Section 18	Continuing Education
71	Section 19	Relaxation & Play
74	Section 20	Hobbies
76	Section 21	Travel Abroad
80	Section 22	Mom U Policies
104	Section 23	Annual Events
107	Section 24	Remember, We Forget

Throughout this guide, you will also find a few sidebars. These are things that happened while I was writing this book. I thought I would add them because when you are a mom, you can't do anything without a few interruptions!

Section 1
Introduction

We have read all the books, asked all the questions and know all the recommendations; but what is motherhood really like? How can we describe it to a woman who is not a mother? I describe it like this: Being a mom is like being a student at a university where instead of a four-year program, you enroll in a program that lasts a lifetime. Like college, you start out with this whole new experience and the possibilities are endless. Just because you are now a mother doesn't mean you still can't follow your dreams, achieve your goals and have a bright future in whatever your aspirations for life may be. Motherhood offers a continuous learning experience and we are constantly experimenting to find solutions to our everyday problems. Being a mom is like attending a Mom University or Mom U.

The Mom U experience is challenging, rewarding, costly and offers a whole new world where we gain valuable life experiences. Not to mention, it can be more difficult than we had ever imagined. Those of you who have attended a college or university know that you meet many new people, learn new things, overcome obstacles, gain weight, experience sleep deprivation, but most of all, have lots of fun! That is what motherhood is like.

Motherhood and student life teach us more about who we are and what we can handle. It gives us a better idea of what we want out of life. When you first get to college, you may experience fear, nervousness and an uncomfortable feeling. Those are the same things you may experience when you first find out that you are to become a mother. But not to worry, as with both, those feelings pass quickly and soon your new lifestyle just becomes second nature.

Instead of late-night parties, there are late-night feedings. Instead of studying for final exams, there are diapers to change, mouths to feed and a little person to comfort. Instead of sitting in class, you are either staying at home caring for your children or perhaps working at a job outside of the home.

Unlike most universities, you never graduate from Mom U. Being a mom is the most rigorous, disciplined and challenging program you will ever join; however, there is no certificate to be earned, no diploma and no place for it on a resumé. Being a student at Mom U is truly the most wonderful experience in the world, and it will offer you more pride and joy than you have ever imagined!

You apply for Mom U once you become pregnant or start the adoption search. After giving birth or receiving a child, you have been accepted into Mom U where you will spend the rest of your life learning, teaching and fine-tuning the art of motherhood. This is not a program you can master no matter how hard you try and no matter how many children you have. The learning process at Mom U lasts throughout your entire lifetime.

Mom U is definitely one of the most interesting and exciting places to be in life. We should never underestimate the power of a child. They have all the power in the world to become what they want to be and to change the future. We just have to learn how to steer them in the right direction, teach them how to use their powers for good, and most of all, teach them respect, compassion and love.

MOM UNIVERSITY

Mom University Student Guide:

Dear Mothers,

    I am pleased to welcome you to the Mom University family. Most student guides start out with some sort of sappy letter about how happy they are to have you (only because you are forking out big bucks to attend) and how they want you to become involved in university life (being a mother, you're sort of involved in the whole creation, birthing, and/or raising process, so I'm pretty sure that counts). Then they go on to say that if you have any questions you can call some 800 number that will get you to a person who will forward you on to another person who will put you on hold for 20 minutes and then get you to a third person who will have to call you back.

    At Mom U, we are all here to help each other out. You can call any number you like and most likely reach a mom. Since I was one of the first of my friends to get pregnant and have children, several of my friends called me for advice. Some of them felt like they were asking dumb questions. When it comes to motherhood, there is no such thing as a dumb question. Each child is different and each will present us with a set of new challenges.

    Again, I am delighted that you will be joining the Mom University community, and we look forward to learning more about you in the years ahead. (What? Did a college or university actually write that?) As a mom, we truly are interested in learning about each other because some moms have really cool tips on stuff.

Sincerely,
Danae Branson

In the following chapters, you will learn about Mom U and its students, departments, athletics, arts and even what a resumé might look like if a mother's Mom U education and experience were to be used. So, for all of you out there applying for this school or those of you who are already enrolled, sit back, relax and enjoy the ride. I guarantee it will be the ride of a lifetime!

Section 2
Students

At Mom U, a student is classified as any woman who takes part in raising children on a regular basis, whether they be biological, adopted, foster, step or inherited. The students at Mom U come from all different backgrounds, including race, religion, age and marital status.

Being accepted into Mom U isn't hard for most people. You don't need a good GPA or even a high school diploma. Your SAT score doesn't matter and neither does your monthly income. Wouldn't it be strange if you really had to apply to a special Mom University, be accepted and then go through their education classes and take their exams before the government would issue you a license to conceive? The reality of it is that some very good moms would probably fail the program. We aren't all perfect human beings and we aren't all perfect mothers. Some of us try to be perfect, but it really is our imperfections that sometimes make our kids laugh, learn and love us even more.

The sad thing is that there are many women who would give anything to have a child but, for some reason, are unable to. Having a child is a privilege and we should be thankful for the little miracles that they are.

As a student at Mom U, there are several different things to consider, such as academics, scheduling, living, childcare, health and safety, finances and support services.

SIDEBAR:

My four-year-old daughter just walked in the room and said, "What are you doing flabby butt?"
Kids do tell it like it is, don't they!

Section 3
Academics

Academics are continuous at Mom U. You are learning 24 hours a day seven days a week. We learn about our children and what works best for them. Every child is different and what works for one child may not work for another. Your first child may have liked to take a bath while your second child absolutely hates water. We are constantly learning new ways to get our children to do the things necessary for life, like eating, drinking, bathing and wearing clothes.

The academics at Mom U are tough, regimented and sometimes tiring. Figuring out how you are going to get enough sleep so that you may function properly is also part of the learning process. My children are two and four years old and sometimes they still refuse to go to bed or they get up in the middle of the night. I have tried reading them bedtime stories, giving them baths right before bed, telling them about the big plans for the next day and even bribing them. I'm sure that bribing is some sort of psychological "no-no," but come on, who honestly has never tried to bribe their child? After all of my trial and error, my own mother finally suggested I try a lullaby CD! My kids' rooms happen to be right across the hall from one another so I put a CD player in the hall between their rooms and it has worked wonderfully! Who knew my own mother knew a thing or two about raising kids? Sometimes we forget the most obvious sources of information.

Sleeping:

My daughter sleeps in a double bed and seems to think that since there is enough room for two people, then there should be two people sleeping in the bed. The other day she said, "Mom, do you think you and dad have saved up enough money to buy me a new sister or brother so I'll have someone to sleep with me?" My reply at this point in time was, "Sorry, honey, but no." So far the lullaby music has sufficed!

Lack of sleep is really most common in the very early years of motherhood when your children are babies. Babies may get up several times during the night for feedings. This can be exceptionally tough for working women. If at all possible, get your husband to help out so you can at least get a good night's sleep once in a while. If this is not a possibility, then hang in there. Your child should be sleeping through the night after a few months. If she isn't, speak with your child's physician. When my daughter was five months old and was still getting up in the middle of the night, I was told that she didn't need a bottle but she was just waking up because of habit. Even though it was heartbreaking, I let her cry through the night one night and she slept through the night from then on. My son was a little different and I had to let him cry for a few nights before he would quit waking up. It may be tough, but hang in there and you'll get through it.

Eating:

Getting young children to eat can be sort of a sticky situation, literally. My daughter eats pretty well and, for the most part, always has. My son, on the other hand, eats like a bird. He gets distracted easily and would rather be off playing than eating. I find what works best is when we all sit at the table and eat together... no television, no phone and no toys. He will sit and eat because the rest of us are. It is much harder to get him to eat in public unless he is starving because there is always so much going on. He will usually take a few bites and then be off and running around again.

I realize I shouldn't worry about his eating, because as my son gets older, I'm sure he'll start eating everything in the house and my daughter will become the lighter eater of the two. Going out to buy groceries is going to become more of a pain in the butt, as I will buying much more food and spending a lot more money. I will just have to keep clipping those coupons and watching those ads. They really should have a special grocery discount card for mothers with teenage boys!

Clothing:

How many of you have trouble keeping your little ones clothed? When my kids were younger, they would run around the house naked all day if I let them. The kids would be outside playing and, all of the sudden, I'd see my son running buck naked through the yard. We, of course, lived in town at that time and I'm sure the neighbors got a kick out of it. My daughter seems to have a problem keeping her pants up. We have tried belts and elastic waistbands, but it seems that she's always got crack! She would make the perfect plumber.

I am not really sure of a good way to keep children clothed. Using tape, superglue, staples or rubber bands would probably just get social services at your door.

Perhaps children will be more likely to keep their clothes on if you let them pick out what they are going to wear. I realize this is a recipe for some hideous outfits, but that is all a part of being a kid. Haven't you ever seen that kid wearing a cape and cowboy boots? It doesn't look any sillier than those kids wearing harnesses and leashes.

Bathing:

The dreaded bath time. Taking a bath is supposed to be fun with bubbles and rubber duckys. My daughter actually likes taking showers now, but I still have a hard time getting my son in the tub. I've tried those bath crayons, which were fun but were really much harder to clean up than they claimed. My mom brings the kids turtle and frog shaped bath fizzies and the kids love to watch them fizzle away in the water. My son, Cody, wasn't sure what to expect the first time he got a fizzy and was very upset that his frog disappeared in the water.

I do have a net bag suctioned to the tub that is full of fun toys. Montana will wash her hair and play with the toys in the shower, but I still have to convince Cody that he'll have fun in the tub once he gets in. When he was very little, he used to enjoy getting a bath in a large cooler or in a Rubbermaid tub when we'd go on vacation. He's getting a little too big for that now.

Listening:

Getting your kids to listen and obey you may be a little harder than you think. Some mothers start telling their children tales about what will happen to them if they don't listen to their mother. For instance, you may tell them that if they play in the street, then they will be squashed like a bug. If they don't bathe, then bugs will start to live in their hair. If they don't eat their supper, then they will shrivel up like a pea. Moms tell their kids all sorts of stories to get them to listen. Some tell their kids that if they sit too close to the television set, they'll go blind, or that if they stick out their tongue, a bird will try to land on it. I even heard one mother tell her children that if they didn't clean their rooms, she was going to put all their toys in a garbage bag and throw them away. She actually got out a garbage bag and started filling it, and boy, those kids starting picking up their rooms instantly.

Lending a Hand:

While we are learning, we are also teaching our children to

become good people. We teach them morals, values, self-esteem and manners, just to name a few. To help my children learn how important it is to do good things, I have them make drawings and crafts for friends and family. We donate Christmas gifts to needy families and our old winter clothing goes to a school for the children who don't have decent winter clothes. The kids also like to pick flowers or bake cookies for loved ones. Recently, we went to play at the town park and it was full of garbage from a baseball game the night before. I told the kids it would be a nice thing to pick up the garbage so other kids could come play at a nice clean park. This was a good way to teach them that it isn't nice to litter. Kids will feel good about doing things for others.

Strangers, Drugs & Alcohol:

Talking to your children about strangers, drugs and alcohol is also a good thing to start early. My very young children know not to talk to strangers unless their mom, dad, grandparents or other close friends and family say it is okay. I don't want them to be afraid of everyone, yet I want them to be careful. They also know about drugs and alcohol. Alcohol is only for adults, and sometimes I wonder if that is even a wise idea. I've told them that drugs are very bad for you and that you should never use them. They are very young, but if you start talking to them early on about it, then you won't just assume they know about them when they get older. Kids these days seem to be exposed to drugs and alcohol at an earlier age than most people ever imagined.

My children also know about police officers. They know police officers keep the town safe by catching bad guys, watching to make sure you aren't speeding and making sure you are wearing your seatbelt. My daughter, Montana, did tell me just the other day that I was driving too fast and the cops would track me down and I would be in trouble. She was in the car with me when I was pulled over for speeding a few months ago. She made sure the whole family knew I had been pulled over by a cop. The funny thing was, both Montana and Cody were sleeping when I was pulled over. When the cop looked into my vehicle and saw the kids he said, "It looks like you've got a couple of dead ones in there." I thought this was a very strange thing for a police officer to say to someone. Nevertheless, he said that since I wasn't wanted by the FBI, he'd let me go with a warning.

It seems as though most of my friends had never been pulled over for speeding until they became mothers. Once you become a mom, it seems like you spend most of your life in a hurry!

Homework:

Once our children get older, we get the chance to relearn much of the things we learned in school when they bring their homework home. We might be surprised at how much we have forgotten since we were that age. Third grade homework may be harder than we think. I don't ever remember having homework until I was in junior high, but teachers are sending kids home with more homework at an earlier age these days.

When the children get into high school, it is really fun to help with homework. We may even need a tutor for ourselves to get through that algebra and geometry.

SIDEBAR:

I just looked out the window to find my husband playing with trucks in the sandbox. My son is sleeping and my daughter is beside me reading books. Who says we ever have to grow up? Sometimes being in your own little world helps you forget about the stresses of real life.

Section 4
Schedules

Scheduling is a part of every education. Making schedules for you and your children may work best for you at Mom U. Children like to have structure and to know what the plans are for the day. Schedules are great, but don't forget to be spontaneous now and again. For the most part, children like to know what time they eat, what time they nap and what time they go to bed at night. Getting your kids on some sort of schedule allows order and organization into your life. Your kids know that every night at 9:00 p.m. they go to bed, and you know that you will get an hour or so to unwind before bed each night.

These schedules are a little different than those we had in our old college lives. Sleeping until noon, eating, skipping class and partying just really don't fit into the Mom U schedule. When you have babies, you'll be lucky if you even get sleep, and hopefully, you'll get to eat breakfast by noon.

Scheduling also prepares the children for school, where they will have definite schedules that they will have to follow for several years to come.

Some of the students at Mom U stick by their schedules so much that it doesn't add flexibility into their lives, which can make things difficult at times. If we don't get home some night by my children's bedtime, then it's not the end of the world. And if they miss a nap one day, it's not too bad. Some children, however, get so fixed on a certain schedule that if they don't get a nap between 2:00 and 4:00 p.m., it totally messes up their whole day and they can become very cranky and just plain difficult to deal with. This goes back to knowing your child and what does and does not work for them. Raising children is a constant game of trial and error. I know how stressful it is when your child gets off his schedule, but it happens to all children and all moms are forced to deal with it.

Activity schedules are also important to keep on a calendar. Color-code your family with a different color for each member. Your calendar will be full of multi-colored appointments, commitments and social events. You'll have basketball two nights a week, dance one night a week, boy scouts one day, a PTA meeting, your niece's birthday party, a work barbeque, a wedding and a Tupperware party. Now you are busy nine days out of the week. Funny, last time I checked, there were only seven! Never fear, mom is here and you'll figure out a way to make it all work, that's what you are best at. Maybe the tenth day of the week will be a day of rest! Oh, if you've forgotten the definition of that word, it means *to relax* or *to take it easy*.

SIDEBAR:

My son just came into my room with a soggy broken packet of silica beads that are often found in shoeboxes, new purses and coats. I asked him if he swallowed any and he said no but that he did have a few of them in his chewing gum. After calling my good friends at poison control, I learned that silica beads are nontoxic and that the only reason they are not to be eaten is because they pose a choking hazard.

Section 5
Living

Living at Mom U is really up to each mom and what her tastes, preferences and finances allow. Some mothers live in nice, well-kept apartments while others live in large, lavish mansions. Each mom can decide what is best for her and her children and what is best for her pocket book. Most of the time, what we want is different from what we can afford.

I know moms who have bought smaller starter homes they plan on living in until their children get a little older. Others live in big old houses that they plan on spending the next several years remodeling, and even others move right into brand new homes.

When it comes to your living arrangements, as long as the home is safe and clean with enough room for a little play, that is really all a child needs. Children are hard on everything, so whatever you live in, plan on replacing things and making repairs as the children grow up.

I don't know how many times I've heard my husband say, "I don't know why we thought we needed a brand new house. These kids just destroy everything!" Well some kids are harder on things than others, and perhaps we just have those kids that have a knack for putting holes in walls, grinding things into the carpet and plugging the bathroom tub with plastic beaded necklaces.

In college, we were able to live in some not-so-great places just because the price was right. Some of those places would not suit the students at Mom U. While in college, I lived in a fraternity house one summer because it was very cheap. It was the most disgusting place I have ever lived as well. There was filthy garbage all over the bathroom floor, severely stained crusty carpet and I'm pretty sure I developed a rash just by sitting on the furniture.

Of course, when it comes to living arrangements, let's not forget a roommate. Some mothers have adult roommates and some mothers do not. If you are one to have a roommate, then this can sort of be like raising another child. You'll more than likely have another person's laundry to wash, dishes to wash, food to make and stuff to pick up. I always tell people that I live with three children. One being two years older than myself!

My roommate is really good about keeping up the yard and taking care of the house. He also does a good job of watching the kids if needed, which I understand a lot of roommates aren't real likely to do unless bribed. In fact, one mother has a roommate that prefers only to watch children over the age of two. Since they have a child that is eight months old, it becomes sort of a hassle at times. Sometimes the roommate may be the one staying home with the kids and caring for them on a daily basis. In that case, he is more than welcome to read this book.

What If I Have Problems with My Roommate?

I wish this issue were as easy as speaking with your RA about the situation and then having them assign you a new roommate, but unfortunately, it's not. There isn't an easy roommate exchange program at Mom U that won't cost you time, money and grief.

As we all know, living with another person can be very difficult at times. To make this a little easier, I have classified roommates into three different categories; Does Nothing, Helps Occasionally, and Does Everything. I am sure you all know which category your roommate falls into.

If he falls into the Does Nothing category, then ask him to help once in awhile. For instance, when he asks you for the remote, say this, "Honey, the remote is at your feet so sit up, move your head to the opposite side of the sofa, reach out your hand and there it is. Now was that so hard?"

We have to teach our children to help us out, why not try to teach our roommates too? If your roommate should ever offer to help you out, then take him up on that offer. If you continue to turn down his offers, he will quit offering. I'm sure there are a couple of other things you wish he would quit offering because you've turned him down so many times, but this "quit offering" stuff only pertains to house work and kid watching. Try giving him a few chores at a time, and you may be surprised at how quickly he could jump into the Helps Occasionally category. If that doesn't work, then maybe you should start giving him a bill for your services. You did the laundry, that will be $50; you took out the trash, $5; charge $15 an hour for cleaning services and $15 per meal you cook for him. I am sure there are other services you could charge him for, but I wasn't going to list all of them.

If he complains about the bill, maybe he should start helping you out once in awhile. If he actually pays the bill then, girl, you can go shopping or to the spa!

We do have to realize that you can't change a roommate, but I believe that you may be able to improve him.

In most cases, it seems fathers have more freedom and can just sort of come and go as they please. Mom U students always have to make plans and arrangements for everything. More than likely, they just can't say out of the blue, "Hey, I'm going to Jenny's house. See you and the kids later." You could suggest that if your roommate start helping around the house more, you won't be so crabby about him doing his own thing all of the time.

If you have a roommate that falls into the Helps Occasionally category, then consider yourself lucky! Keep thanking him for helping out and still ask for help on occasion. This is really the best you can hope for from most men, and after talking to your friends who have Does Nothing roommates, you won't think your roommate is so bad. A Helps Occasionally roommate will still ask you to look for something for him that he hasn't even tried to look for himself. He may also be one to ask you to schedule certain appointments for him and then be mad at you when you didn't schedule them right. Yes, all roommates can be hard to please.

I'm not sure if a Does Everything roommate actually exists, but anything is possible, right? We can still keep dreaming. If you do have one of those rare Does Everything roommates, then do nothing; I repeat, do nothing. You got a great thing going and don't ruin it. You may think you can push for more, but it might backfire on you and then you'll be back to a Helps Occasionally or even a Does Nothing roommate, and you'll be kicking yourself for screwing up!

SIDEBAR:

My son is looking at himself in the mirror while putting earrings up to his ears. I see he is wearing one of my necklaces and a bracelet. We just won't let my husband know about this, okay?

Section 6
Dining

Dining at Mom U can become somewhat of a hassle if it's not planned properly. Some mothers take time each week to prepare a menu so they know every day what the meals are going to be. This really works slick, especially if you still have children needing bottles and baby food, because they tend to take more time during the meal hours. When the kids get a little older, even if you know in the morning what you'll be having that night, you can lay food out if necessary, and that way at mealtime you're not struggling to find something to eat.

In college, it was great just to go eat at the food service where everything was ready to eat and the variety was limitless. Food Scurvice, as we called it, really wasn't that bad, all you had to do was show up and eat.

Eating out is also a fun thing to do on occasion. Some mothers and their families eat out more than they cook at home. Others of us get the chance to go out only once in a great while, which makes it more of treat. Whatever you choose, the options are there. Do whatever fits best into your lifestyle. Stereotypes say that mothers are good cooks. Well, I'm sure you know a few whose children would starve if mom were doing the cooking every night. If you're lucky, your roommate will pitch in with the meal plans as well.

Children going to school will eat lunch and sometimes breakfast away from the home. These are usually well-thought-out, healthy meals and are of limited portions, unlike at college were you can eat whatever you want when you want. This is why most people gain weight when attending college. I gained 20 pounds my freshman year when living in the dorms, and then lost it that summer when a couple of friends and I moved into the fraternity house and worked in our college town for the summer. Since we were in charge of buying our own groceries, poor college kids tend to lose some pounds.

Section 7
Transportation

Moms and minivans have become a big deal over the years. Minivans offer great room and comfort for traveling, attending sporting events and running errands. Moms with several children need more room to tote their kids and all the stuff that usually goes with them. You'll find that as a mom with small children, the house goes with you wherever you go!

Minivans aren't for everyone, though. Some moms prefer SUVs or cars. SUVs are sporty looking and can provide the same room as a minivan as well as four-wheel drive, if needed. I have had a minivan and an SUV and really liked both. Living in the country in Iowa, however, an SUV with four-wheel drive is almost necessary.

Cars are still being used as the family vehicle. Right now, they are so much less expensive, get better gas mileage and some still have comfortable room for five. Growing up, my parents only ever had cars. There were three of us kids and we sat in the backseat on several long trips and family vacations.

Dealerships now may offer you 24 hours to use a vehicle to make sure that you are choosing the right vehicle for your lifestyle. Have you seen the commercials...? Every big decision deserves 24 hours? Just picture yourself leaving the hospital with your brand new baby. As you leave, you tell the nurse, "I'll try this out for 24 hours and then I'll get back to you." How many returned babies do you think the hospital would get? Probably none, because everyone would be too dang tired to drive back to the hospital the next day.

In some cities, moms may take other forms of transportation such as a taxi, subway or bus. Whatever the transportation, there are several ways to get around. If you are traveling in your own vehicle, always remember to carry your proof of insurance, driver's license, registration, and try not to speed. Again, it seems that moms are always in a hurry and getting pulled over only wastes time and money. Besides, speeding can lead to accidents that could've been easily prevented. It's better late than never.

Section 8
Childcare

Most universities deal with some sort of childcare. At Mom U, we all deal with the decision of whether to work and take our children to a daycare provider full-time, part-time or not at all. To each her own in this matter. Some women are just unable to stay home with their children due to financial reasons, career aspirations or because they just can't stand staying home everyday. That may sound harsh, but we aren't all wired the same way and some of us need adult conversation or time away from our children in order to keep our sanity.

Part-time work would be an ideal situation for a lot of mothers who want to be able to spend more time with their children but also feel the need to continue in a career and have some adult contact throughout the week. We all choose our own path, and a lot of us make sacrifices to be where we want to be.

Staying home with your children does allow you to spend valuable time with them, time that you will never get back. Some mothers have to tighten the budget in order to stay home or some may even decide to watch other Mom U students' children to make some extra cash. There are several opportunities out there for women to stay home and work. If they are very good at multi-tasking, which most mothers are, then they can have the best of both worlds—income and more time spent with their children.

There are several options, and we all do what is best for us. Finding good daycare can be hard and you should always go with your gut. I found some daycare providers that seemed like they probably did a good job caring for children, they were in a convenient location, the price was right, but I just had a strange feeling in my gut about them. I never settled for a daycare provider because I couldn't live with myself taking the kids to someone that I felt uneasy about. If you aren't sure where to take your child, get references from other parents who have had good experiences with certain providers.

Interviewing daycare providers can be quite interesting. My husband and I interviewed one provider who told us that her cat liked babies so he would jump up in their cribs and he only bit them on occasion. She also told us that she wouldn't feed our daughter baby cereal because she thought it stunk. She then proceeded to tell us that sometimes she'd leave the kids alone with a nine-year-old while she ran errands. I guess I was thankful that she was so honest, because I probably would've taken my children there had she not mentioned the above three things. Needless to say, this provider never watched my kids and no longer does daycare.

Daycare horror stories only make moms more nervous and we shouldn't have to worry about our kids all the time. Children are resilient, and once they get old enough to talk, they will tell you more about their daycare than you ever imaged. I had some pretty terrifying experiences with daycare providers when I was a child, and I turned out okay. At least that is what my psychiatrist tells me.

Section 9
Health & Safety

Health and safety are extremely important aspects of attending Mom U. We all want our children to be safe and to be in the best health possible. A lot of mothers feel like their kids are sick all the time. As soon as they get over one sickness, they've got something else. Just a little tip I've learned: when your child gets over a sickness, make sure to wipe down doorknobs, light switches, toys, book covers and anything else that gets touched regularly, with a sanitary wipe. The remote, phone, faucets, refrigerator handle and toilet lever are other items people tend to touch regularly. I also buy new toothbrushes on a regular basis too, just to eliminate being re-infected with sick germs.

I have run across some children who seem to get every unheard-of virus and infection possible. These kids tend to get diseases you thought were only found in animals. Usually children do outgrow this phase, which is very comforting to know.

Make sure that your children stay up-to-date on their check-ups and vaccinations. Most children are seen about five times for well-childcare checkups and vaccinations before age two. After that, most children are seen once a year thereafter with the majority of their vaccinations being completed before age five.

Watching your child get a shot isn't the most pleasant thing in the world, but these shots are saving their lives. My daughter just got her last round of shots before she can attend school. She was very upset and begged me never to take her to the doctor again. Getting shots at one year is very different from getting them at four years.

Along with staying healthy is eating good nutritious food. Children should really get a well balanced diet from the five food groups, with occasional treats. I mean, really, who doesn't give their kids treats once in a while? That is all part of being a kid. It is also my thinking that moms deserve treats too, because we are also kids, right? We all had to come from somewhere.

Sometimes it is just plain easier to give our children junk food because of our hectic schedules, so try to have raisins, cheese, carrots or granola bars on hand. A little healthy food is better than no healthy food at all. When it comes to food, we are teaching our children eating habits that they will carry with them into adulthood. It seems as though childhood obesity is rising and I would prefer my children not have to deal with that. They will probably have to deal with acne-prone skin in adolescence, thanks to me. Unfortunately, we can't pick which of our genes get passed on to our children.

At Mom U, it is also very important that you take care of yourself. Fortunately you are out in the real world and at Mom U we have good doctors and clinics to visit. You won't have to visit "Student Death," as we called Student Health in college, or listen to all the horror stories about doctors who don't really know what they are doing by removing the wrong body parts, prescribing the wrong medications or actually making you sick when you just went in for an annual checkup. Well. I suppose maybe we still read these sort of stories in the paper, so make sure you research your family physician and clinic before trusting them with your lives.

Safety, another important issue, is also a concern of many of the students at Mom U. Child seats, outlet plugs, cupboard locks, toilet locks, drawer locks and baby gates are just a few of the safety items that we all rush out to buy once we have children in the house. You will have to teach your roommate how to use these items, and chances are, your child will figure out how to work them before he does. My kids were always pulling the outlet plugs out of the outlets, opening locked cupboards and climbing over the baby gates. We try to childproof our homes as much as possible without installing padded walls and bubble wrap. Let's face it, our kids could find a way to get hurt on a pillow. Kids are kids and they come with a lot of bumps and bruises.

My daughter has had her fair share of ouches, but she seems to be learning from her mistakes when it comes to boo-boos. My son, however, either loves getting hurt or isn't the brightest crayon in the box. He could ride his bike down a hill, wipe out and get back up and try it again. Did I mention that my son is only two and that he has no control over bikes going down hills?

At Mom U, we may learn that safety regarding boys and girls are two different ball games. Girls are usually smart enough not to climb up on the back of a chair until it falls over and then try it again. But like I said before, all kids are different and sometimes it just doesn't matter what the gender of the child is, being a daredevil is just in their nature.

My poor son looks like a walking accident. He has bruises on his legs, arms and once in a while he will sport a black eye. He could be walking and then purposely fall just because he thinks it's fun. If there is a patch of ice, he will slip on it; if there is a barbwire fence, he will run into it; and if there happens to be a needle in a haystack, he would be pricked by it. I guess you could say that we support the families of the makers of Band-Aid and Neosporin. If a kiss from mom doesn't heal the pain, then a neon-yellow ice pack shaped like a racecar always does the trick.

No matter how accident-prone your child is, a car seat can most definitely save his life. It seems as though the law now requires your child to ride in a car seat well into his thirties but they do this for your child's safety. Children are small and frail and need to be secured in a moving vehicle. I don't quite understand, however, why a child has to be in a car seat or booster seat until age six, yet they can ride at age four in a school bus without a seat belt? Inquiring minds want to know.

Along with child safety is teaching your child emergency numbers as well as knowing the emergency numbers yourself. 911 is the most common emergency number to call, but if your children are like mine, it may also be a good idea to add poison control's number to your speed dial. I think the people at poison control know me by name.

SIDEBAR:

My son just asked if I could get him his own phone book because he needs to make a few calls.

Section 10
Finances/ How much will it cost me a semester?

The answer to that question.... A lot! Funding your education at Mom U may not be an issue for some mothers, but may be a huge concern for others. We all want to make sure that we have enough money to get through our own education as well as pay for our children's. Besides food and clothing, we may have to pay for formula, diapers, daycare, school, cars, college and weddings, just to name a few.

We will want to take our kids on vacations, they may be involved in music, drama, sports and clubs that may be costly at times. There will always be extras here and there that we didn't count on and you may find that one child is more expensive than another. Your daughter may require more clothing, jewelry, hair spray, make-up and facial cleansers than your son. In the other sense, your son may want stereo equipment, Game Boys, four-wheelers and larger more expensive items than your daughter.

A lot of us want to provide as much as we can for our children, but we shouldn't let it get out of hand. Our child does not need every toy in the world or need to wear the most expensive clothing. Mothers with little money may be doing what they can so their child can be dressed to the hilt, but some of the wealthiest moms buy their children's clothes at garage sales and second-hand stores. In case you've forgotten, the clothes will get dirty, they will get stained and the kids will outgrow them. As most Mom U students have found, toys can become dust collectors instead of entertainment. Children can only play with so many at a time and I've found that the more toys, the more clutter. As long as you can feed, shelter, clothe and love your child, that is what matters most. There is no need to go into major debt just so your kid can have every toy on television.

Your child will be just as happy playing with plastic lids and cardboard boxes as they would with the latest talking, singing, walking doll.

Growing up, I don't ever remember having friendships based on our parents' salaries, but perhaps in some areas of the world, the rich stick with the rich, the middle class stick with the middle class and the low income stick with the low income.

I do have mom friends today that are worried about whether or not they can buy their kids name-brand clothing once they get to school. They remember all the popular kids wearing expensive clothing in their high school. This is really a sad aspect of life; we all want the best for our children, but is teaching them that having the most expensive of everything really the answer to popularity, or life, for that matter?

I guess this is part of what being a mother is about. We will be dealing with issues that we tend to forget when our children are young. Once our kids get into school, we will be dealing with their education, sports, their friends, puberty and all the fun stuff of growing up.

Section 11
Support Services

As with most colleges and universities, Mom U offers support services. By being a mom, you can get support from family, friends and professionals, if needed. Most of us are surrounded by other mothers who can offer advice and there are several parenting magazines and other books out there that can help you with your journey through Mom U. Just remember, not every answer is the right answer for you and your children. This is like science class; we are continually experimenting and hoping that once in a while we get things right!

Just for your own peace of mind, there will be days when you want to scream, cry or possibly run away. When you go to college for the first year, you have to adjust to the change. You'll be away from the friends and family you love and you will experience independence, responsibility and possibly loneliness. It takes time, but you do adjust to your new lifestyle.

As a mom, you don't just have to deal with the challenge to adjust in the first year, but in every year there after. Children grow and change and you have to adjust to them in every stage. Some mothers have to adjust to caring for more children than they are used to and some may have to adjust to caring for fewer children than normal. No matter what you are feeling, someone else out there is feeling or has felt the same way at one point in time. If you need help, then get it, and remember that there are always better times to come. You'll wake up one day and be a grandmother, and I've heard that this stage in life is where the real fun begins!

SIDEBAR:

I just went to check on my daughter, who is doing a few dishes in the kitchen. She starts pre-school in a few days and is very excited. She told me that she is going to make lots of friends at school. I told her that was great, but I didn't want her to forget her best friend: her brother. She said, "Cody isn't my friend, he's my brother." I told her that Cody could be her friend and her brother and she replied, "But sometimes he hits me, kicks me and screams at me." I reminded her that she isn't always nice to him either. "Well, come this fall I am going to be nice to Cody because since I am going to school I will be all growed up," she explained. As if attending school magically turns a small child into a mature individual!

Section 12
Visitors/ Prospective Students

Mom U has several visitors and prospective students each year. We try to accommodate them by exposing them to motherhood and even asking them to help out. My sister visits Mom U quite often and still hasn't made the decision to apply yet. She has decided maybe in a few years she will be ready to enroll. Some women will decide that Mom U is not for them, and that is quite all right. Mom U isn't for everyone, it's just for thrill-seeking individuals like ourselves.

For many women, visiting Mom U can actually be a very effective form of birth control. I mean, if you aren't used to being sleep deprived, controlling screaming kids and having everyone and their dog watch you while you pee, Mom U could be a rude awakening. Mom U is not for those with weak stomachs, because as a mother you are at times forced to do things to your child that you would never do to yourself. You may have to stick your finger down their throat or use a Q-tip covered in petroleum jelly to help them out when they are constipated.

I remember being a visitor to Mom U. I remember thinking how much work it was, how gross it was to see kids with snotty noses and watch mothers change poopy diapers. I watch my friends who don't have kids with my children and you can tell that they get annoyed and irritated by them at times. The kids run, jump, play and interrupt our conversations with questions, needs to go to the bathroom and hands that need washed.

Having children isn't an inconvenience, it's a privilege, and the positives to raising them are endless. Hearing that little voice say, "I love you, Mommy" or "I need you." Seeing the excitement in their little eyes when they see you after a day at the babysitter. Having them snuggle with you in the early morning or reading them a book at night. Listening to them reading books to their little brother or being so proud of themselves because they drew you a picture or picked you flowers. Knowing that they feel safest in your arms. These little people are truly the greatest gift a person could ever receive and that is all the more reason why a woman should be one-hundred-percent willing to enroll into Mom U before applying. You will never be a hundred-percent ready for Mom U, but you should be a hundred-percent willing. If you aren't willing to give your child everything it deserves, please remember there are families out there that will.

Visitors will come and go and some will enroll and others will not. We like visitors because then sometimes we get a break and they help out with the kids! If you are just a visitor to Mom U, please ask a student to give you a tour or presentation on what life at Mom U is like. If you decide to become a student then great, if not, perhaps you could still offer free babysitting.

Prospective students are those that are pregnant or in the process of getting a child. In both cases, the child hasn't arrived yet. These women will become students no matter what, so there is no turning back. These women need lots of encouragement and support and any woman at Mom U should be more than happy to give that to them.

One thing I would suggest to Mom U students when giving advice to a prospective student is focus on the positives more than the hardships. I mean, sure these beautiful little people can drive you crazy, ruin your things and leave skid marks in their underwear, but so can your husband, and half of you have kept him!

Most prospective students are nervous to have their first child. They aren't quite sure how they are going to handle caring for such a tiny person. They think things like, *What if I don't feed it enough? What if it never sleeps? How am I going to take it places?* Most moms just sort of know what to do when they have that baby. You will hold that baby in your arms and the answers just magically appear. When in doubt, just ask questions. I know I called both my mom and my mother-in-law several times after the birth of my first child.

Besides caring for a new baby, most new mothers are nervous about the pain of childbirth. I have two words for you epi dural. Epidurals are great, so I'm told. I didn't have the pleasure of an epidural with either child, but they will take away the pain so you can relax and enjoy the birth of your child.

Attending Mom U isn't all chocolates and roses. I mean, you'll run into a few nuts and thorns along the way, but that is life no matter whether you are a mom or not. There will be sleepless nights, screaming, crying, and after you can get your roommate to calm down, you'll be able to get some sleep and take care of your baby better!

Unfortunately, no one can prepare you for how difficult Mom U is, but if it wasn't something we could handle, then no sane person would ever have more than one child, right? We all need to remember that worrying doesn't accomplish anything or solve any problems. Everything seems to have a funny way of working out.

Section 13
Orientation

Being pregnant is like orientation into Mom U. You will most likely read books or ask questions that will help you adjust to motherhood. One fun thing to do in orientation is decide on the baby's name. Emily, Emma, Jacob and Michael are among the most popular names today, but moms these days are getting more creative. Famous moms tend to name their kids very unique names such as Rumor, Apple, Pilot Inspecktor, Denim, Ryder or Jett. Why not try Silo, Tin, Evian, Era, Cheer, Napkin, Shelf, Knot, Apron, or Panorama? Instead of naming your kids after objects or name brands, why not spell your name backwards and see if there are any possible names. For instance Pam would be Map, Lisa-Asil, Angelina-Anilegna, Niki-Ikin, Sarah-Haras, Megan-Nagem and the list could go on and on. I always thought Nadia and Aidan would be cute names for twins because they spell each other backwards.

Chances are, no matter what you name your child, you will call them by some sort of nickname. We call Montana - Baby Cakes, Flips, Tana or Missy. Cody is usually called Chunky Buddies, Code Man, Wild Man or Codero. Other Mom U students call their kids Peanut, Pumpkin, Sweetie, Sugar and I've even heard some use Bacon or Slim for nicknames.

Whatever you decide to name your child, just remember that this is the name your child will have the rest of his life. Also remember that your child is going to be a grown up someday and Dr. Napkin Jones just doesn't have a great ring to it.

Picking out a nursery theme is also a fun thing to do during orientation. Some mothers go all out with fancy curtains, lamps, wall borders and stuffed animals in pinks or blues depending on the sex of the child. Others just have a bed for the child and not a particular room of its own. We chose to do our nursery in colors that would work for either sex so we wouldn't have to redo it in the future.

Section 14
Books

Of course we need books to get through our Mom U education. I don't mean books about being a mom, I mean books to read to your children. Many children's books are very interesting and even if my kids get bored half way through the story, I will read the end myself because I am interested to see how it ended.

These books are a little different than some of the college textbooks we have read. The difference is these children's books are actually very interesting and they teach the children very good lessons and how to use their imaginations.

Also, the nice thing about children's books is that you don't have to take a test over them when you are finished. Unless, of course, you are just reading the book without fully paying attention to what you are reading. Your kids will ask you questions and you'll have to re-read it to answer them. My kids have several books and some are their favorites, and others we haven't read much, but for them, reading those books is a great source of entertainment. They especially like it when I give each character a different voice. I found this keeps their attention longer than if I just read it in my normal voice. Reading books to your children can be an excuse to try out different accents.

The cost of these books is also considerably less than a college textbook. Plus being able to read several in a short amount of time gives you a stronger sense of accomplishment!

SIDEBAR:

I just heard my daughter ask her brother if he would like to play hide and seek. My two-year-old son replied, "Not now, I'm trying to get my work done." He was pretending to fix a toy truck. I guess there are many times that work can always wait because playing with your children will not be a luxury that you'll have forever.

Section 15
Colleges and Departments

Now that we have learned some about Mom U, the students here, and how you go about visiting or enrolling in Mom U, it is time to discuss the colleges and departments. At Mom U, you will study several different majors including discipline, foreign language, education/ethics, organization, business, babies, toddlers, adolescence, young adults.... And those are just a few!

Discipline:

Along with motherhood comes discipline. We not only have to be disciplined ourselves but we have to discipline our children. We need to teach them that there are consequences for unacceptable behavior and every mom will decide on her own what type of discipline she is most comfortable with. Part of a mom's being disciplined is following through. When you tell your child that if they hit their sibling then they will be punished, then follow through. Children are smart and they figure out ways to get around being punished and soon the mom may not be able to control her own children. Lazy parenting usually causes bad behavior in children. Do what works best for you and your child, just don't let the child walk all over you because disciplining them will only get harder as they get older.

It does seem that I could scream at the kids until I was blue in the face and there are days when they would still misbehave. Yet, a little holler from their dad and they shape up in an instant. Either their father is scarier than me or the kids tend to grow too comfortable with me. You'll notice for the most part your kids will be perfect angels for their grandparents, aunts, uncles and the occasional babysitter. If your children go to a regular daycare provider, chances are they will grow comfortable with her too, and after the first few weeks of regular care, their true colors will start to appear.

I will be the first to admit that I am very uncomfortable disciplining my children in public, so I tend to let them get away with more. The kids catch on to this quickly and start to behave worse in front of others because they know mom isn't going to be so harsh on them. I have had to find a way to punish them in front of others without looking like a 'mean' mom. I usually take them aside and have a little talk with them. For the most part, this works well, especially if they are having a good time and you threaten to take them home if they don't start behaving.

Foreign Language:

Many moms speak to their babies in what we call "baby talk." Some moms become so good at "baby talk" that they even use it when talking to adults. This type of language just has a way of taking over, and before you know it, you are calling just about everyone honey, sweetie and schnookums. Some moms even make up words for things, much like children do. There are some conversations I've had with moms where a translator would've been nice.

Learning to understand a child learning to talk can also be a bit difficult. Moms usually understand their child even though their language may be foreign to everyone else. My children would combine words to form their own. For instance, my daughter would combine buckle and tuck to form the word "tuckle." She would put a belt on and say, "Mom, can you tuckle this?"

Over the years, my son liked to look through "noculars," my mother-in-law had her "goal blodder" removed and we all would take a drive in the "behicle." The cute little accents of a child are plenty to put a smile on your face. These accents fade all too fast and soon they are learning words so fast they could surprise you everyday.

Education/Ethics:

Educating our young ones is very important. They will go to school and learn a lot, but they won't learn all of life's little lessons at school. Parents usually are the ones to teach their children good manners, the importance of being kind to others and not to steal, lie or cheat. Things like that are often learned from their parents, as well as the good examples their parents set for them.

This can be very tricky because we tell them never to lie, but they may catch us in a lie. Perhaps as a mom, the kids went shopping with me and I bought a pair of new shoes but asked the kids not to mention it to their father. Things like that are hard to work around. In most cases, it is just best to be honest with everyone; however, we, especially as women, are all aware of when the truth can hurt and a little white lie sometimes isn't bad. For example, when your best friend gets a new hair cut that you dislike, you'll probably tell her that you like it when she asks. So you didn't like her hair, no one has to know that but you and would you really want to make her self-conscious or ruin her day by telling her that you don't care for her new style? Probably not. However, I do have friends who are very honest and will just flat out tell you they don't like your hair. We all just have to realize that not everyone is going to like everything about us. And that makes them weird people, not us!

For the most part, kids will pick up on those things as well. I guess if we have, then they will in time. Remember, we were kids too. Some moms tend to forget that they were also children once. This may help you out more than you know. You have experience being young, carefree and playful. Somehow a lot of these memories must be erased during childbirth.

We all want our children to be kind to others, so we must be kind to others as well. There are people out there who are less fortunate than us and it is great to show some compassion. You know how you feel about your children; look at everyone as someone's child and perhaps your feelings will change towards them. That jerky guy at the office has a mom that loves him more than anything, the crabby woman down the street has a mom who would do anything for her and even your boss was somebody's precious baby.

Organization:

What would life be like without organization? Motherhood, I mean chaos! Organizing your life and keeping it organized are two different things. Try to keep calendars and lists, plan menus, assign chores and do a little cleaning each day. To keep up, do one load of laundry every day, pay bills on a set day each month, and get rid of clutter and useless objects.

It seems that we are all packrats and we have closets and drawers full of things that we NEVER use but we save just in the tiniest chance that we will need it in the future. I bet you would all be amazed at the things you've kept over the years. If you start looking through your closets and junk drawers, you could have a few good laughs as to what you find. In one of the closets in my house, I found coats that we never wear, an old bottle of shoe polish we bought three years ago and have never used, a golf ball (and we don't golf) and some brand new valances I bought on clearance for my kitchen a few years ago but never put up. I even found a Chia pet, remember those?

In the junk drawers, I would imagine that half the stuff you find you won't even know what it is or what it goes to. Instead of throwing things away, a lot of us like to save things because we think we will use them at another time. These items just take up space and add clutter. It never fails though, you'll throw away all of your useless junk and then for some freak reason you'll need one of those items two weeks after you got rid of it. You'll then wish you would've saved those old shoes, that dress that was too small and that old bottle of glitter hairspray.

Part of the organization education is making a few extra bucks by having a garage sale or donating your unwanted items to a secondhand store! I love garage sales because I can find good quality, hardly-used clothing for my kids. Kids grow out of clothes so fast or wear them out that I hate to spend a fortune on them. Besides, my kids have butterfingers and tend to spill on themselves quite often. Stain stick does wonders, but sometimes it just isn't a match against my active kids.

So make a day and clean out the clutter! It may be more fun than you think.

As moms, we realize that no matter how organized we are, we still tend to have those days where we feel like we cleaned the living room 12 times, washed the same clothes twice and swept the floor every other hour.

Let's face it, we aren't all organization freaks and some of us don't care to be. There will always be a mess, sometimes it's better to leave it for later and just play with the kids. Kids grow up and move out but messes will be around forever.

Business:

Mom U students often learn that being a mom and business go hand in hand. Whether you are a stay-at-home mom, work from home, or work outside of the home, business education is essential. Stay-at-home moms are running their own businesses. They supervise others, assign tasks, provide support, oversee projects and make sure that the whole household runs smoothly. Running your own profitable business from home or working outside the home also involves a great deal of business skills.

Staying at home:

Staying at home takes great discipline, patience and often financial support. This is a career that a lot of women would love to have but cannot afford. If you were to stay at home until all of your children were in school and then went looking for a job out of the home, why shouldn't you be able to add your Mom U education and work experience on your resume? A stay-at-home mom's resume may look something like the one on the following page.

Danae D. Branson
1234 Vine Street
Any town, IA 66578

Personal Profile:
Hardworking, organized and dedicated professional with knowledge of human relations, early childhood development, first-aid and home management.

Education:
Student of Mom University
February 2000 to Present

I am becoming a well-rounded individual with knowledge of just about everything under the sun, from medicine to education and communication to security.

Professional Experience:
Childcare Specialist, Branson Household
February 2000 to Present

My duties include making sure the household operations run smoothly by overseeing all of the cleaning, clothes laundering, culinary arts and buying. I am in charge of all the finances including the budgeting, paying bills and miscellaneous expenses. I delegate tasks if necessary, conduct negotiations, motivate associates and am in charge of associate training. I have managed several different personalities and am an efficient worker on little to no sleep.

I act as the in house physician, nurse, teacher, maid, cook, nanny, financial planner, shopper, garbage woman, chauffer, psychiatrist, musician, drama queen, secretary, insurance agent, media specialist and security guard.

Hobbies:
I'm sorry, hobbies? I don't have time for hobbies, but if I did, I would like to learn to play the guitar, learn to Salsa dance and learn to speak French.

Being a student at Mom U doesn't mean that you can't have a profitable job inside or outside of the home. Your career schedule, goals and aspirations may change once you are enrolled in Mom U, but there are several options to go with.

There are part-time jobs, telecommuter jobs, jobs that have on-site daycare and jobs where you may only work a certain season. The Internet, career fairs and networking with other working Mom U students are great places to start to find the perfect career to fit your schedule. Remember, it's not always what you know but *who* you know. You'll be surprised what type of opportunities you can find just by talking to people.

Some jobs are filled by referrals only. There are positions that aren't advertised, so if you want something, it never hurts to ask. Go out and get what you want, you may not get your dream job right away, but never give up. Eventually you will find what you want and it will be worth the wait.

Don't give up on your dreams just because you are a mom. Still try to sing, write, play music, play sports or invent something. I always wished I was a good singer and I would try out for American Idol. I am sure a lot of us sing in the shower or the car and think we have the best singing voices. I've seen a few moms on American Idol and the latest winner was a mom. I wonder what the judges would think if I took a tape of me singing in the shower into the audition because that is, of course, where I sing best. I could use a hose and showerhead on stage to perform and if I win then perhaps I could have a shower in the recording studio. I can just hear one of the judges, "You've got to be bloody kidding me!"

Arts:

Being a student at Mom U opens your eyes to a wide variety of arts. Did you ever consider washing dishes or folding laundry an art? Well it can be a creative process because we all think of creative ways for them to get done or creative ways to get someone else to do them. We are also creative about juggling things and doing multiple tasks at once. Wouldn't you consider folding laundry, changing a diaper, reading a book and talking on the phone all at the same time a form of creativity?

The great part about the arts is that children love them. Start your kids in the arts as young as possible and don't fret if they don't do things perfectly because neither do we. My daughter loves to unload the dishwasher, fold her own clothes and organize her room. I've made these things a fun exciting thing to do. We turn the radio up and dance while we work and then we get a special treat when we are done. Also, just knowing that her father is going to be "so happy" when he finds out how good she's been is a great reward for her.

Folding clothes is actually a very easy job for children to do and who cares if they don't do it right? It will get put away, pulled out and worn again, so how it is folded isn't that big of a deal.

Also dusting, vacuuming and sweeping can be an art. I give my kids dust clothes and they wipe down the furniture, but their favorite thing to do is washing windows. They have so much fun spraying the windows with window spray. Of course, you need to be very careful of any cleaner you give your child, so I use only safe cleaners in my home.

But let's be realistic, I couldn't get my son to clean his room if my life depended on it. I've offered helping him, I've tried bribing him and I've tried making it a game like "let's see who can pick up toys the fastest." He isn't interested. He just says, "You do it, Mommy." I have to pick up after his father, why not him too!

Cooking can be very creative. Trying to find new dishes and different foods to try can be difficult. If you are like me, you probably cook the same 10 dishes over and over again. I finally dug out the cookbooks I had received as wedding gifts, birthday gifts or whatever and started trying new recipes. Some of them turned out great, some of them we'll never try again and some of them I made by accident. One night I was going to add chili powder to fish batter and accidentally added cinnamon instead. It really wasn't that bad. I also try to get the main bulk of our groceries once every four or five weeks since I have to drive 45 minutes to the grocery store.

Have you ever tried to take your kids to the grocery store? I swear, when I walk into a grocery store, the employees are thinking, *Oh, no not that lady and her kids again*. I have those kids that run off, pout because I won't buy them candy and fight over who gets to ride in the cart. The one thing I've also found interesting about grocery stores is not only do they have the candy and gum at the front of the store but now they've added toys. I wonder if they do this so the kids will beg their parents for a toy and just to keep the kid quiet the parent will buy the toy making the store money or if they do this knowing parents won't bring their kids in if they have to buy them a dang toy every time.

The kids and I try to plan menus and I always clip coupons. It usually seems that there just isn't enough time in the day to get things done. If I'm in a crunch for time, I will be doing things while sitting on the pot or while I'm eating. Now if that isn't multi-tasking, then I don't know what is!

If you can master the art of always having something fun for your kids to do, then you have come a long way. Kids have all these toys and half the time they won't play with them. I have found that large boxes, laundry baskets and empty toilet paper rolls can be super-fun toys.

My son has a lot of art on the walls in his room. He has drawn on the walls with crayons, ink pens and he even took a toy plastic hammer to the corner of one of his walls and chipped off a few pieces of sheet rock. He has been disciplined, but kids are kids, and you will find wonderful art just about everywhere.

My son has smeared poop all over the woodwork in the bathroom, peed on the front door, drew on the kitchen floor with a marker and thought that Silly Puddy would make for a nice hair gel. My daughter used Desitin as a face paint, smeared hot pink lipstick on our carpet, gave herself a hair cut one week before my brother's wedding in which she was a flower girl and painted the babysitter's living room with finger paints. It only takes two seconds for your little one to become a creative little artist.

School-aged children will hopefully have plenty of the arts in school to be involved in. They'll be bringing home papers full of glued-on macaroni, pipe cleaner animals and clay pots. Then they'll join a music class and practice their singing while in the bathroom or decide they want to play an instrument and will be tooting their horns on Sunday afternoons while everyone else is resting.

It is a great joy to see your child performing in plays, dance recitals and concerts. They are so proud of themselves, and you should be very proud of them as well. After all, they could become the next big singer, actor or musician.

Music as a mother may be a little different than the music you were used to listening to in college. You may go from rocking to the Beastie Boys to listening to lullaby songs or Barney. My children love Barney and other fun children's songs, but they also like pop and country music. They have their favorite songs and I enjoy that music as well. Especially on long trips, it helps to listen to my favorite music while driving. If your children love their kiddy music, then let them listen to it and when they fall asleep change it to your own favorite music.

Athletics:

A lot of students at Mom U are interested in the athletics. We offers several different options to choose from, such as the Child Chase, Pick Up, Clean & Clean Again, Wrestle to Dress, Stair Climb and Rush to Pee.

We also offer everyday activities like playing, walking, swimming, bike riding and floor exercises. You can just about make anything a workout. Besides all the cooking, cleaning and playing, I try to get a 20-minute walk in five times a week just to clear my head or dream up writing projects. I also enjoy Pilates because it is low cardio and I can do it with the kids around. They even lie down and exercise with me. Sometimes this isn't so great because they seem to think that I can exercise while they are sitting on top of me.

Strollers are great to put the kids in and get out for a walk. The fresh air will do everyone good, and it may make the kids sleepy, which is always a plus!

Athletics may become a big deal in your house once your child gets to junior high and high school. You can practice shooting hoops, playing catch or volleying with a volleyball. These sporting events may become so fun you won't know what to do once your children all graduate and leave the home.

Some parents even get into coaching their child's sports teams. Keep in shape by doing some of the practice workouts with the kids. You'll gain their respect and lose some extra pounds that way.

Babies:

Some of us love the area of babies. Babies are soft, cuddly, and after a nice bath and some baby lotion, they smell so good. They sleep a lot and only drink breast milk or formula. Some babies prefer the presence of your company at all times, which can lead to some interesting nights.

Babies also like to get ear infections and gas. It's amazing how much gas build-up a small person can have. I believe it's just one of those inherited genes from their father.

Smiling, cooing and wiggling around are also favorite things for babies to do. They love it when you talk to them and they love to bounce and move around. I remember my daughter used to wiggle so much that she'd wiggle right out of her diaper. I learned that Velcro-fastened diapers would stick to her clothing and come off very easily. I decided to stick with the sticky fasteners and she had a lot less messes that way. My husband actually nicknamed her "Flippy" because she was always flipping around.

Babies change and grow so much and writing about their experiences was one of my favorite things to do. I keep journals on both the kids so I don't forget how fun each stage of their lives are.

I try to write in their journals about every two weeks. I chart their height, weight and what new things they are learning. It's fun now to look back to see what life used to be like when they were babies. The sleep deprivation, constant diaper changes and nightly feedings can be easily forgotten once your child grows out of that stage. It's refreshing to see that my journals do reflect the best times because I know there were times when I thought I would lose my head if it weren't screwed on.

Once my son was born, it was fun to look back in my daughter's journal to see how the kids were different. Cody slept five hours a night right off the bat compared to Montana's two hours. Cody has remained a pound or two heavier and an inch or two taller at every stage. One of these days he is going to be bigger than his sister, and boy is she going to be in for a rude awakening.

I've heard some people say they would have more kids if they'd remain in the baby stage while others say they'd have more kids if they could skip the baby stage.

I love to hold babies, but I do like to give them back to their moms when they get upset or need a diaper change. I have plenty of bottoms to help wipe at my own house!

Toddlers:

Babies grow up and become adventurous toddlers. The terrible twos aren't so terrible. Okay, who am I kidding, they call them the terrible twos for a reason. They are learning, exploring and sometimes just trying to help out. This is that age where you have to watch them 24/7 because they can literally get into everything, crawl into everything and get stuck anywhere.

At this stage, you are having all sorts of potty training experiences and possibly dealing with kids that bite. The potty training can be quite interesting. My kids have pooped in the tub, smeared poop on their legs and peed on just about everything in the house. Once we even found our son molding his poop into balls and putting them in his sister's toy oven. You would think these children are animals.

My kids were little rascals at this age and very different from each other as well.

Montana wasn't too thrilled about sharing my attention with her baby brother. She pulled on his arm one day and said, "Baby go bye-bye, baby go bye-bye," as she pointed to the door. Both kids were in to everything. I felt like all I did was chase them around and clean up the dirt from plants, the pots and pans from the cupboards and the toilet paper that they would unwind.

As soon as one mess was cleaned up, another would be in the works. Cody has a knack for spilling everything and the floor remains in a sticky state. I sweep and mop and repeat but the floor just remains like one of those sticky fly traps.

Montana has always loved reading books, organizing her toys and picking out her own clothes. Cody enjoys ripping books, breaking toys and emptying his dresser drawers. I guess that is the difference between a boy and a girl. Cody has always been a bit more rough and likes to wrestle and climb things. Montana likes to color, make beaded necklaces and wash the dishes. Yes, she loves to wash the dishes! I am sure in a few years that will change.

This is also the age were they are learning new words and talking more and more every day. My son's favorite word right now is "nipple." Yes, you read that right. Don't ask me why, but he'll just walk around the house saying, "nipple, nipple, nipple." I'm not sure he really knows what that word means. He also talks with that little kid accent, so at times it is hard to understand him.

He woke me up one morning around 7:00 a.m. to ask me to get him his "barrows." I couldn't understand what it was exactly he wanted, so I asked him to explain. He started getting frustrated because I don't know what "barrows" are. Montana walked in, and if all else fails, she usually knows what he is talking about. That is the nice thing about siblings, they usually understand each other when no one else does. Unfortunately this time she wasn't sure what "barrows" were either. He kept saying they were in the Jeep. Finally I remembered him playing with some rubber bands the day before, and sure enough, that is what he was talking about. How he got "barrows" from rubber bands, I do not know, but at least we figured out what he was so politely asking for.

Kids will come up with all sorts of words and ask all sorts of questions. This is the age where they become great entertainers. These little people are so much smarter than we think. They say things that will amaze and even shock us. They will also say things that will make us want to crawl into a hole for the next ten years.

Adolescence:

Now this can be a very fun age. They are becoming adults and going through so many changes. They are worried about acne, puberty, popularity, athletic ability, their looks, weight and the opposite sex. All the experiences we had at that age come rushing back, and to relate to our children, we remember what we went through and how we felt at that age.

These children are slowly becoming adults and can become rebellious.

My children have not reached this age yet, but I remember myself at this age. I thought my parents were strict and unfair at times. I also would do things just because they didn't want me too. I realize now how glad I am that they disciplined me so well and just didn't let me run wild. I had curfews and had to tell them where I was going and who I was going with. There are certain things that I would've never done, no matter what, for fear of disappointing my parents. I wish how they handled my sister, brother and me at that age could be bottled up and sold. The three of us turned out okay and I know someday I will be forced to deal with rebellious teenagers.

I also remember having acne, braces and glasses during this time in my life. I was picked on because of my looks in upper elementary. I eventually grew out of this stage and started feeling better about myself. Now I just worry about cellulite, stretch marks and adult acne. I wouldn't want to do adolescence over again; every stage of life is a new experience and always seems to be better than the last.

Young Adults:

Now our children are grown up and it is time for them to leave the nest. A lot of mothers have a hard time letting go after the last one leaves to college and the "empty nest" syndrome may set in. We just have to have faith that we did the best we could raising our children and that they will be able to live their lives to the fullest and make good decisions. We are raising future Mom U students and, I guess, Dad U students too.

We will still learn to deal with our children as they age and have children of their own. We may not always agree with their lifestyles, but it is their lives, and by this age, they really will do what they want. We all have to make mistakes to learn, and we all make mistakes. I'm sure our mothers may not agree with some of our life choices, but we all try to move on. It doesn't matter how old your child is, you will always be their mother. I know seventy-year-old moms who still want to ring their forty-year-old child's neck. Some of us never outgrow that pesky child stage.

SIDEBAR:

I just checked on my daughter who was in the shower in her bathroom and then checked on my son who is taking a bath in my bathroom. My son had blood dripping down his face and I asked him what happened. "I was shaving like Daddy," he said. The child had gotten a hold of my razor and tried to shave his upper lip. Fortunately he only had a small cut on his lip that was revealed after I washed away all the blood. Even after having children in the house for four and half years, I still sometimes don't think about every little thing they can get in to.

Section 16
Hardcore Years

Hardcore years at Mom U are the years where the children are living at home with us and/or are being financially supported by us. We may think that our tensions will ease and our stress levels will decrease when our children leave home to start their new lives, but we will miss them terribly and probably worry about them more because we won't feel as involved in their day to day lives.

A lot of times, women get stuck on how many years they want children in the home. Some people are okay with one child, others prefer two, three, four or more. The students at Mom U all have different reasons for having the number of children they have. Some students know exactly how many kids they want and others of us are stuck with that nagging question: "Should we be done or should we have another?" It seems to me that a lot of people want the same number of children that their mother had. If you only had one sibling, then you may only want two kids; if you had two siblings, you want three kids; and so on. Of course, if you came from a family of eight, you may not want that many.

I have two beautiful healthy children but I have been debating whether or not to have another one for the last year or so. Four people seems to be a nice sized family, and I wonder how one more would affect our lives. I have two siblings and thought it was fun that there were three of us growing up together. However, many times it comes down to how many children you can handle and still feel comfortable with your sanity level. Finances also play a huge factor. For now, two is all we can comfortably afford and I would love to give my two everything I possibly can.

You can talk yourself in and out of this decision for years. Sometimes we just need to make a decision and stick with it. Of course, juggling three children is harder than raising two, but two is also harder than raising one.

When having children, you just do what you have to do. Everyone does what they feel is right for them, and a lot of times, even today, people are surprised when they learn that they are having a new baby.

If you are having a problem deciding whether or not to have another child, look at the things in your life that would have to change. Is pregnancy covered on your health insurance? Does your daycare provider care for newborns? Is your home or vehicle big enough to accommodate another child? Do you have plenty of cash flow to live comfortably with another child?

Another thing we should really look at, no matter how many children we have, is getting our financial affairs in order. Making sure we have enough life insurance, a will and trust are also very important. Setting up retirement funds for ourselves and college or wedding funds for our children may also be a good idea.

Retirement savings is so hard because most of us need that money now! It's hard to save for the future when the present seems more important. It seems strange how we work our tails off to make money and raise children and then when our children are out of the home, we start to retire. We finally have the time and money to do some traveling and fun things, but our children are already out of the home doing their own thing. I guess nobody ever said that life made sense.

These hardcore years are typically the most stressful. I was at work the other day picking strands of hair off my sweater. I commented to a co-worker that I was losing hair and jokingly said, "I wonder if I have some sort of disease?" He, being a father of three, replied, "Yeah: motherhood." I've never considered motherhood a disease, but it does remind me of those drug commercials.

Motherhood can cure loneliness, boredom and bring meaning to your life.

Motherhood is not for everyone.

Please consult a physician before considering motherhood.

Motherhood may cause side effects such as nausea, vomiting, irritability, mood swings, stomach cramps, back pain, hair loss, blurred vision, weight gain, fatigue, insomnia, skin irritations and bleeding gums.

If you experience any of these side effects, just get used to it.

SIDEBAR:

I am ready to scream. My son just spilled chocolate milk all over the floor and then decided he had to go poop. Well he didn't make it to the bathroom, and there is poop all up his back, on the floor and on the toilet. Then my daughter decided to fill a bucket with water, sand and dead grasshoppers. I just found the bucket in the house, and there is also an old bird's nest floating in it. To make matters worse, my husband is mad because someone reset the odometer in his truck. Some people only wish that is the only thing they had to worry about!

Section 17
Extracurricular Activities

As with any university, there are several extracurricular activities to be involved in at Mom U. You may have birthday parties, weddings, showers, picnics, barbeques and several other events to attend. The difference is now that you are a mom, you either have to figure out whether you are taking the children along or getting someone to watch them. When you have really little children, you usually have to move the whole house to go anywhere. Once the kids get older, they don't require so much stuff on outings.

Community Involvement:

Once your children get older, you may feel the need to participate more in school or community programs. You may decide to be on the school board, go to PTA meetings or join your town's chamber of commerce. Whatever you decide, being involved may not only change the future of the town and its educational system, you may just meet some great new friends.

Section 18
Continuing Education

    Some of us decide to go back to school after we've become a mother. This is more difficult than going to college right out of high school; however, by now you probably have your head screwed on straight, and you will probably actually do better in college as a non-traditional student than you would as a traditional one.

    Accomplishing this education may mean more to you, and you may have a greater determination for it now than you did before you became a mother. You are not just bettering yourself, but you are working towards a goal that will affect the future of your family. My parents decided to go to college to get their bachelor's degrees when I was in elementary school. My dad started college when I was in kindergarten and my mom started when I was in second grade.

    They studied after we went to bed at night, took night classes and worked full-time. They both graduated in the top of their class and went on to get great jobs because of their educations. I, on the other hand, went to college right out of high school and since I didn't have the sense of responsibility that my parents had when they went to college, I tended to be a social butterfly my freshman year and my classes weren't as important to me. I got involved in so many extras, like intramural sports, clubs and committees, that I barely had time to study.

    My freshman year of college was a huge growing

experience for me, and by my sophomore year, I was ready to buckle down and try harder. However, I learned quickly that no matter how hard I tried the next few years, it was hard to recover from that first year.

I actually have a friend now who has two children and is going back to college to get her bachelor's degree. She really wasn't too bright in high school; you know, she was one of those that didn't even know who the first president of the United States was at age sixteen, but is doing great in college because she is really trying hard to get a higher education so she can get a better job to help support her family.

You will do what you have to do to make your continuing education work. After having children, there really isn't anything we wouldn't do for them.

SIDEBAR:

I went out to the living room to check on my kids. They are playing with trucks on a play rug. I sat down and asked my son how he was doing. He complained because my foot "touched" his rug. I then asked him for a hug and he gave me one saying, "Now you can leave me alone." Well if he doesn't sound just like his father....

Section 19
Relaxation & Play

Mom U isn't all about work, work, work!!! We all work hard, so we deserve to play hard. Having children gives us a chance to be kids again. We get all sorts of cool toys to play with, we can swing on the swing set again, go down the slide, jump on a trampoline, play in the play lands at fast food restaurants and play in the rain.

The last time my husband and I took our kids to a fast food restaurant, we all played in the play land together. We timed each other to see who could make it through the tunnels and slides the fastest. I had bruised shins the next day, but it was worth it.

Why not play in the rain, jump in the mud or build forts? It's time to be a responsible parent, but it's also time to live a little. A little dirt never hurt anyone, and having fun and letting go will allow you to relieve stress.

Sometimes the kids and I just turn the radio up and dance. I love singing and dancing to fast music and we have a great time dancing and laughing together. Sometimes while the kids are in the bath, we make up songs to sing to make bath time more fun. One I sing to get my son in the tub is something like this:

It's bath time chica boom boom chica boom boom chica boom boom
(repeat twice)

Now take off your clothes and get into the tub (clap, clap)
(repeat twice)

It's silly, I know, but the kids and I have fun with weird songs.

I think it would be fun just to sit in a toy store with them and play with the toys in the aisle like all kids like to do. However, I imagine seeing me sitting on the floor in a store playing with toys may look sort of strange. Why should kids get to have all the fun?

In the winter, we love sledding, building snowmen and making snow forts. In the spring and summer, we go fishing, swimming and love playing with the hose. I soaked my kids with the hose while watering trees the other day. They giggled and laughed, and it's only water, right?

The kids and I also like to do tricks. I'll flip them over or they'll balance their stomachs on my feet. I also give them rides on my back and then I flip around like a bucking bronco. Of course, I'm very careful and so far no one has gotten hurt besides myself. They are starting to get too big for that now though.

If you can get time to yourself, then read a book, lie in a hammock, go for a walk or soak in the tub to relax. Sometimes "alone time" is good, if you can remember how to deal with yourself, that is.

Just relax in general…. The kids are going to spill, they are going to break things, draw on things and ruin things. They will puke on the carpet; they will pee the bed; and chances are, they'll get some sort of food on your brand new outfit right before a big night out. It is all a part of being a student at Mom U, and guess what? All Mom U students go through it and understand that's life!

I haven't gotten around to getting my kids' baby books done or their scrapbooks started, but I have been good about

MOM UNIVERSITY

writing in a journal for each of them. I write about the funny things they do or say, how big they are getting, what size of clothing they are wearing, how many teeth they have, when they first learned to roll, crawl, walk and talk and many other things. Even though my children are only four and two, it is still fun to look back at how they used to be and someday they'll enjoy reading those journals too.

SIDEBAR:

We are on vacation—yes, I even write on vacation—and Montana asked her grandmother, "When I grow up, will I still be your grandkid?" Her grandmother replied, "Yes, and when you have kids, you can bring them on vacation with you." Montana said, "Nah, that'd be too much work." Who knew a four-year-old could say it all!

Section 20
Fun Things for Moms/ Hobbies

There are several things that we can get involved in and enjoy. If you love decorating your home, then make a hobby of it. Read interior design books, try new and interesting decorating themes and save your money to buy the items you want for your new hobby.

Gardening is also something fun that a lot of moms love to do. Planting flowers or vegetables is also something the kids could enjoy. You can now brighten your house with fresh flowers and make fresh salsa with the vegetables in your garden.

I would love to take my sister and mother on a spa day. Going to the spa to relax and have others pamper me would just be the greatest thing right now. Believe it or not, my four-year-old daughter does like to put lotion on our feet. She is like our little foot massager. She does get a little out of control at times, and you'll have to use the lotion that she has put on your feet for your legs and arms, but its fun.

My girlfriends and I still have a sleep over once a year. We all get together at someone's house with no husbands or kids and we give ourselves pedicures, facials, watch movies, read magazines, eat food and, of course, just chat. We have so much fun and it is a blast to act like silly teens again. Usually the next morning we will go shopping or catch a movie. None of us get to the theater much anymore, so we will pick a fun chic flick, sit back and enjoy.

Many moms have gotten into scrap booking. Scrapbooks are great and you can make them as elaborate or as simple as you want. Some mothers get so into scrap booking that at the rate they are going they are going to have to purchase a small trailer to store all the scrapbooks they have made! Start a scrap booking night with your friends once a month and feel like you are accomplishing something while you socialize.

Section 21
Travel Abroad

Perhaps as a mother you want to explore the world. We live in a world of constant change where occurrences in remote corners of the globe profoundly impact our lives. Chances are, we won't be traveling too far with small children. Traveling with children can become quite interesting. The vehicle will be packed full of toys, clothes, and fun gear. We always pack the kids games, coloring books and toys to play with to make the trip go faster for them. I also pack drinks and snacks for them. We usually stop a few times for bathroom breaks, but my kids have surprisingly large bladders. I probably use the restroom more times a day than they do!

That whole "are we there yet?" question can get quite annoying. I've thought about just answering them with a "yes," pulling over, letting them out and then driving off. That would be mean, but I bet the look on their faces would be priceless. I would, of course, go back and pick them up!

I have yet to experience flying with my children and am pretty sure my son would love it, but my daughter would probably be scared to death. Of course, if you can get them flying when they are young, you may have less problems with that later on. My children will probably get the chance to fly when they are older and we can afford the price of plane tickets. The real problem will be getting my husband on a plane. He is not real fond of flying.

We have thought about taking the Amtrak to our vacation destinations. There is beautiful scenery and you can eat at a table and sleep in a bed if needed. That may be fun to try once for something new and different.

When your kids get a little older, it would be fun to take them to far-away places to expose them and yourself to different cultures.

Every year I get excited to go on vacation. I look forward to relaxing, doing fun things and just hanging out. I know I won't worry about laundry, dishes, cleaning, work or paying the bills. Every year we get to our vacation destination and after the first day I realize, "who am I kidding?" I am a mother of two small children, so even while on vacation, I have to deal with the day-to-day duties of being a mother. I have only moved the fighting, kicking and screaming to a new location and threw in a zoo and an amusement park or two.

Sometimes I think time away from your kids allows you to appreciate them more and that is why I have friends who take vacations without their small children. Being away from them gives you a chance to miss them, and you'll look forward to the great things about them again. On the other hand, taking your children on vacation may allow you to spend valuable time with them. Growing up, the children will remember the good times on the family vacations; or at least, you will.

I am told that a lot of children hit an age where they no longer want to go on vacation with their parents. It's that age where they become embarrassed to be seen with mom and dad. I think this happens around junior high and could possibly last through high school. At this age, the only thing more embarrassing than being seen in public with parents is being forced to wear matching outfits in public with their parents! When I was a senior in high school, my whole family took a vacation to Colorado. My grandma got us all matching t-shirts to wear while we were out sight seeing. I was eighteen and had the attitude that I didn't know any of the people in the area anyway so it didn't bother me to wear the same shirt as everyone else, but my brother and cousin who were both in junior high had very different feelings on the subject. They did wear the t-shirts, but they wore them under sweatshirts so that they couldn't be seen. They would've rather roasted in a sweatshirt in the Colorado summer than be caught wearing identical shirts with the rest of the family. A lot of other families actually commented on how neat it was that we were all wearing matching shirts. So, to those junior high kids in those families, sorry!

If your older children aren't so excited about going on vacation with you, then you and your husband can probably use some much-needed alone time and go without them.

Exchange Program:

Mom U doesn't offer an exchange program because we are afraid too many mothers would take advantage of it. I'm not sure how it would work, either moms would be able to move to another country while leaving their family behind for three months or perhaps it would involve exchanging the children for different ones. I guess it may be something to think about. Just recently I did see a reality television show about trading spouses. I don't think that would really be for me. If you are having a hard time living with someone you've known for years, then what makes you think it would be better with a complete stranger? I guess if you are looking at experiencing a new culture, then look into housing a foreign exchange student. This would add one more child to your home, but what's one more kid, right? This child could teach you a lot about their culture and perhaps you could go visit them some day.

SIDEBAR:

My husband and the kids are sitting in the living room watching television. I heard my daughter yelling "stop, stop, stop" several times. I figured since she was yelling and I didn't hear her dad say, "quit your fighting kids," that he was picking on her. Sure enough, when I went out to check on them, her father was putting is foot on her leg and she was yelling "stop." Then he'd pull his leg away and do it again. I suppose some of us never quite outgrow that urge to pick on people.

Section 22
Mom U Policies

There are several things you will find at Mom U that do, in fact, happen to just about every student.

Phones:

Your child will be perfectly good until the phone rings. You'll pick up the phone to talk to your best friend, mother or whomever, and it is almost guaranteed your child will need your attention, start screaming, want a snack, need to go pee or suddenly hurt himself.

I am wondering if phones don't put off some sort of telepathic signal to kids and a voice rings in their head saying, "bother mom." It could happen. Most students at Mom U will learn to help their child while talking on the phone, but there are times when it is just best to get off the phone and hope next time your child won't be affected by the piece of plastic you are holding up to your ear.

Just recently, my daughter decided to climb the dresser and get into my jewelry while I was on the phone. While I was talking, she fell off the dresser and needed me. My dresser is really short, but it scared her. I've also caught her up on the counters and climbing the windows when I've been on the phone. Sometimes I feel like I live in a zoo.

Good Clothes:

It also never fails that your child will either spit up on you or wipe food or dirt on you when you are wearing a new or nice outfit. Good clothes are magnets to kids. Wear your grungies around all day and the kids won't touch them. Put on a nice black dress and a pair of hose and pretty soon you're covered in dirty fingerprints.

Spills:

Kids love to spill. This is one of their favorite things to do. They will stain their clothes, the carpet and anything possible. A lot of kids are chronic spillers. You could be wiping up one spill and they've already spilled again. That is why sippy cups were invented; however, some children will figure out how to spill out of those too!

Crayons, Tape & Scissors:

Children are fascinated by these items and I would bet that any time your child gets a hold of these, something other than paper will be colored on, taped or cut. Walls, tables, floors and furniture make great canvases for little artists to create on. Scissors are great for cutting clothing, doll hair and real hair. When I was little, my mother was taking a nap on the couch and my little brother got a hold of a pair of scissors and decided to become a barber. My mom woke up with a new do, and to this day, I'm not sure we could find those scissors, even if we tried.

I used to draw cookies on the wallpaper and blame it on my little sister. I still have a sweet tooth. See, we are now moms, but we used to do the same things that we get upset with our children for.

Accidents:

Accidents *will* happen and they are inevitable. This is all a part of growing up. I actually know adults who are probably more accident prone than their kids! We can't be too hard on the kids for these things. I try not to get my panties in a bind over too much. I laugh when I probably should be crying, but laughing I have found relaxes me more than crying does.

Just the other day, my son got some Febreze out and doused the entire laundry room in it. When I asked him why he had done that, he replied, "It was dirty, Mom. I was just cleaning." How can you get mad at a child for helping you clean?

One of the kids accidentally broke my very expensive vacuum cleaner. One accidentally got gum stuck under her armpit. They seem to accidentally hit each other a lot and my son seems to get accidentally bruised, scraped and bumped quite frequently. He is that child that stands straight up on the seat of a bicycle to see how long he can balance.

These little people we are raising are constantly growing, changing and exploring the world. Most of them seem fearless.

Mealtime:

As a mother, you will learn quickly that if you get to eat with the rest of the family while the food is still warm, you should consider yourself lucky. I don't know how many times I've finally sat down to eat and the kids and my husband are already done. Somebody always needs something, even if you think you've covered all the bases and everything in the kitchen is sitting on the dining room table. At least now instead of eating cold food you can always stick your plate in the microwave.

Embarrassing Moments:

Some of us do a great job of embarrassing ourselves in public, and once we become mothers, we don't need some punk kid coming along and worsening matters in any way. My daughter wet her pants one day in the grocery store, and before I realized what had happened, she was standing at the end of an aisle with only her shirt on. She was holding her shoes, jeans and underwear in her hands. I didn't have a diaper bag, so I did the unthinkable. I made her put her wet clothes back on so I could take her to the car and change her clothes.

My son once threw a tantrum at the checkout counter because I wouldn't buy him gum. He also asked a shoe salesman once if he was his dad. My daughter has yelled, "Mom, that lady has a mustache," in public and has also told women that they are "flat chested." These "flat chested" women were very surprised since they all happened to be well endowed. Once I explained to them that for some odd reason, she thinks that "flat" is the same as "fat," they completely understood. So, in essence, she was calling these women "fat chested." My kids have also de-pantsed me in public, which was really nice.

Children will embarrass you along the way and some probably will never stop. I'm sure there is a sixty year old out there who is still embarrassing her eighty-year-old mother.

Moms and Appearance:

Most moms become self-conscious of their bodies. They may develop stretch marks, cellulite, the front butt, and some claim that they get hairier. There are so many strange things that can happen as a result of pregnancy. With my son, I was unable to wear my contacts for months because the pregnancy changed my eyesight. I've also heard of women who develop problems with their teeth and gums as a result of pregnancy. This baby is literally sucking you dry! I know I am definitely not in the shape I was in high school, but the kids are worth it!

I do what I can though; I exercise, eat right, drink plenty of water and slather on the cellulite cream. I could save up for laser surgery to remove the stretch marks, but I just don't see that happening. My children sort of need underwear and shoes first. Really it isn't so bad. Things can always be worse right? We should all be thankful for what we do have.

Weight seems to be the most sensitive subject around moms. I remember when my daughter was four months old, a friend of mine asked when I was due. Well if that didn't get me out exercising the next day. Most people know not to ask a woman when she is due unless they know for sure that she is pregnant! Many of my friends have tried Weight Watchers after giving birth, and that seems to work wonders. I did have a friend that lost weight by eating mostly doughnuts and chocolate shakes, but I believe she is just a freak of nature!

It seems like in college you gain the freshman twenty, the sophomore thirty and so on. When you become a mother, there seems to be the mandatory motherhood weight gain and this usually comes after the mandatory marriage weight gain. You would think we would be losing weight as these children typically run us ragged!

Another aspect that seems to go along with motherhood is the urge to cut your hair. The "mom" haircut is one that most of us try when we are pregnant with our first. We also wear maternity clothes way before we need them and we just want that baby to get here yesterday. By the second child, we have started growing our hair back out, we wait until the buttons on our jeans are popping out before we switch to maternity clothes, and we aren't as anxious for the birth of the second.

We are actually more nervous about how we are going handle two kids. I've heard that if you go on the have a third, chances are you may still be wearing maternity clothes since the birth of your second and your older two children will end up raising that child. This child becomes more like the family pet and everyone chips in to do their part!

Children's Questions:

Children will come up with the strangest questions ever imaginable and it is important that we do try to answer them, whether we know the answer or not. My two-year-old son asked his four-year-old sister what the thing between his legs was and she responded by saying, "that's your tail." Now my son talks about his tail and how his dad has a tail. The other day, he asked me if his dad ever plays with his tail. Well how do you go about answering that one?

Children will almost always touch your chest and ask what that is also. I tell them, those are called breasts, everyone has them, and please don't touch them. They will inevitably learn the word "boobies" and next time they see you naked will say to you, "Mom, I see your boobies." Why is it kids pick up on that type of stuff? You could try for weeks to teach them the alphabet or their colors, yet it takes them two seconds to learn the word "boobies" and what it means. My daughter was actually very distraught to learn that some day she will develop breasts. She cried and cried and said she wished she were a boy. If she inherits that trait from me, then she won't have anything to worry about.

My kids also talk in strange languages, shake their booties and make funny faces. Isn't it funny how children can act like nuts and people think it's funny, but if I were making funny faces at people, shaking my butt and talking in gibberish, I would probably be committed to a padded cell and put on twenty-four-hour watch.

Kids also ask why, why and why again. You'll be surprised because some of the questions they ask we won't be able to answer, because frankly, we don't know. A lot of the questions, however, we may get a chuckle out of.

The other day, Montana asked me if clouds were made of sugar. I knew the answer to that one... no! She often asks questions like, "How does a rainbow appear?" "How does a car run?" and "What does a cop do?" Riding in the jeep last week, she asked what kind of animals had shells. I told her that turtles, snails and clams all had shells. Cody added in his two cents and told her that tacos also had shells.

Mirrors:

Both my kids like to sit in front of the mirror and talk to themselves. Or they will be in my room looking at themselves while they are talking to me. It is so funny to watch them do this. My son will turn his face to the side and to the other side and my daughter will dance in front of the mirror. I think a lot of adults are like this though too. If you've ever worked in an office with a mirror, you'll catch people nonchalantly looking at themselves in it. They check out their teeth, their noses and the back of their hair.

Imaginations/Creativity:

The older we get, the less creative we become. Children can be a true inspiration, and at Mom U, they teach moms that you are never too young to dream. You can also create an interesting path for yourself through life. Kids can come up with the most unique ways of doing things and they are always thinking outside the box. Think outside the box. How can we provide for ourselves? How can we become successful at doing something we love? And how can we make a great life for our children? These are all questions we ask ourselves daily, and sometimes we don't come up with any answers.

Let your child be a child as long as they can. They grow up too fast, and before you know it, coloring outside the lines becomes unacceptable. You can color a picture whatever color you want. Why can't a person have blue hair and purple eyes? Why can't a skunk be red and yellow or a horse be pink? Sometimes we try so hard to teach our children the "right" way to do things, we suck all the fun out of it.

The other day, my daughter wanted to make herself a sandwich. She put butter and mayonnaise on two pieces of bread and called it lunch. That was what she wanted, so I let her eat it; she has also made raspberry jelly and ham sandwiches. I'm not going to tell her that it's wrong. I'm not going to let her eat candy and cookies all day because that just isn't healthy, but otherwise, she likes to be creative with her food. My son is quite the opposite, he could live on peanut butter sandwiches if I let him.

Mom U and raising kids makes you appreciate the little things in life; the little things you may have taken for granted before your life revolved around the little people you helped create.

Advice:

Students at Mom U have learned a lot and I have compiled some of the best advice ever given to moms out there like us.

- Sleep now and clean later.
- Take people up on their offers to help cook, clean or watch the kids. If you always turn them down, they will quit offering.
- Be silly with your kids.
- Don't be afraid to make a mistake in front of your kids. Now they will know that you are only human and that nobody is perfect.

- Read to your kids, play with your kids, hug your kids and rock your kids while they are young, because someday they'll grow up and won't need that anymore.
- If the kids want to help you cook or clean, let them. They get the feeling of teamwork and who cares if they don't do things the "right" way? At least they get done.
- Your children should come before your work. Chances are, work will still be around in eighteen years, but your children will be off to college.
- Spoil them rotten when they're too young to notice.
- Listen to your children; they need your attention.
- Spend special time with each child individually, you really get to know them better this way.
- Eat snow, dance in the mud and climb trees, people think it's less strange if you are doing this with children than alone.
- Get used to taking your children with you almost everywhere. The more you take them out with you, the better they learn to behave well in public.
- If you want cellulite cream to work, then you do have to apply it twice daily.
- Just because you're a mom doesn't mean you have to dress like one.
- It's not fun to be so serious all the time… laugh, smile and dance.
- Once you have children, the word "privacy" no longer exists. Get used to peeing before an audience.

Smarts:

Most of us find that kids really are smarter than we think. They learn about things that are good and bad for you, they learn relationships, and they learn loyalty at a young age. My kids stick together, no matter what. They can hit and kick each other, but no one else can.

One day Montana had a stick in her mouth. I asked her to please take that stick out of her mouth and she told me that it wasn't a stick, it was a cigarette and that she was smoking. I was so shocked, but she has relatives and family friends that smoke, so of course she would know what that is.

Last year my dad came to help my husband, Ben, put in a new furnace in our house. Montana was glad to see her grandpa but was a little upset that grandma didn't come too. She got on the phone to talk to grandma and said, "Your husband came to visit me, but you didn't come." I guess maybe she was more than a little upset.

Montana and Cody love tools. One night, Ben and I were cleaning the basement and Montana and Cody were using screwdrivers on the tool bench. Montana wanted our attention so she yelled, "Daddy, look, Cody and I are screwing!" Ben and I about lost it.

Learning new words can be really tough for children. Just the other night, Ben, being the big deer hunter that he is, was teaching Cody the words fawn, doe and buck. Cody seemed to get confused and combined the "f" in fawn with the "uck" in buck. We were very pleased to know that he doesn't yet know this word or what it means!

Boogers:

At Mom U you will learn that kids and boogers go hand in hand. They all seem to pick them and they all seem to eat them. Now I will admit that as a small child I had an occasional bugger snack or two. I also liked to eat glue, but couldn't really tell you why. It sure didn't taste good.

If the boogers don't go in their mouths then they will pop up all over the place. I have found boogers in their hair, in the blankets, on their clothing, on my clothing and on the furniture and carpet. Too bad boogers can't be used for something good, because these little snot factories sure do produce a lot of them.

Worms:

There is a large supply of worms at Mom U. Most little boys love to carry these crawly creatures in their pockets or in a bucket. My son calls them snakes and refers to them as pets. He wants to make sure that they eat dirt, drink water and have plenty of sticks to play with. He likes to find mommy worms and baby worms and keep them together. Once he claimed to find a brother and a sister worm, which made him very happy.

Lying:

Children start to tell fibs and make up stories early on. My daughter once told her great grandparents that a guy wrecked his car in our ditch and that the cops had to come and get him. We, to this day, aren't sure why she would make up a story like that, but that is the mind of a child. I have noticed that telling stories may become worse in some children reaching adolescence. The lying, and even stealing small items, becomes something of habit.

Montana likes to blame things on her brother when she knows that he didn't do it. I was the oldest child and I did blame things on my siblings even though I may have done them. I would even hit my sister or brother, my parents would see me, and I would still say I didn't do it. Maybe this is part of a child's creative mind; I don't remember really knowing at such a young age that my lying was really a bad thing.

I had friends in early elementary who would steal little things from each other like Barbie clothes, dolls or small change. It seemed to them that if you wanted something and could sneak it out of your friend's house, then it was yours. This is one of those things that a lot of children go through but a lot of students at Mom U don't realize it. For the most part, we did a lot of the same things our children will be doing, and if we didn't, then someone we know did. Those are the things we forget.

Medicine:

Most children hate medicine. Mothers have tried for years to find easy ways to get their kids to take medicine. Chances are, you have bibs or shirts that are stained with bright red medications that your child spit out all over the place. Ask your doctor if you can mix the medicine with some type of food or drink. Since my kids have gotten a little older, I almost always try to find chewable tablets that they take a little better.

Big Deals:

Kids tend to make a big deal out of the smallest things. With two, they think everything has to be the same. If Montana eats her macaroni and cheese out of a bowl, then so does Cody. If he gets to drink pop out of a can, then so does she. If Montana gets to sit on my lap, then so should Cody. Some things are just natural with the kids, but other things we try to compromise. They still like their own sets of toys. She is the typical girl with Barbies, dolls and kitchen sets. He plays with trucks, dinosaurs and tool sets.

Growing up and keeping things even-steven across the board can become somewhat of an obsession for some kids. I never sat at Christmas and figured out how much money my parents spent on each of us kids; I never counted presents at birthdays to make sure that when my birthday came around I'd have the same number of presents as my sister; and now that my siblings and I are grown, I don't get upset if my parents help them out in some way but don't help me. I'm sure there have been times when they helped me out and not my siblings.

Some people I've heard keep track of every thing their sibling may get that they don't get. They count gifts, figure up costs and make sure that their sibling isn't ahead of them in any department concerning the parents.

Sometimes your child may make a big deal out of a wrong colored glass or because you gave them a spoon instead of a fork. To a child, almost everything could be a big deal. The older they get, the more they will relax about this sort of thing because they will start to have more to worry about rather than if you gave them a blue sucker instead of a red one.

There are a lot of things your children will not learn or understand about you until they become a parent themselves. Then it will be like a light bulb going off in their brain, and suddenly throughout the years, they will understand more and more about why you did the things you did raising them.

They Learn by Watching You:

Kids really do learn by watching you. They learn how to brush their teeth, comb their hair, eat, put on make-up, write, and the list goes on and on. When my daughter was two years old, I went to set her on the little potty chair and she had a mini pad in her underwear; she learned that from watching me. Or the day she put make-up all over her face and then decided to do her Barbie faces; she learned that from watching me.

My son has learned a lot from watching his dad. He thinks he needs to pee outside, he wants to rake the yard and he wants to hit things with his hammer. Children learn so much and they imitate all the time. It can be very cute, but at times it is difficult because we have to be careful of what we do and say. They also become little echoes. They can pick out a swear word in an instant and those will be the words they repeat. It's like they are born with the knowledge that certain words are bad.

Competition:

In most universities, students are constantly competing for top ranks in their classes, special awards and honors, athletic positions, music positions and theater roles. Competition among Mom U students just simply shouldn't exist when it comes to being a mom. Mom U students are one big team of mothers experiencing the same life-changing issues day in and day out. We should all be lending an ear, offering support and helping each other out. Of course, as a part of life and the real world, we compete for jobs, government offices or a place in organizations, but we shouldn't compete for who is the better mom. We are all good moms in our own special ways. It's just like the old saying goes… it doesn't take one person to raise a child, it takes a village.

Doctor's Advice:

I was watching the news the other night and saw this doctor who was talking about how children are very similar to Neanderthals. They use emotion, gestures and strange noises to communicate. Plus, they are messy. Anyway, I was thinking that this doctor is pretty dumb to assume that, as mothers, we didn't figure out that if we marry a Neanderthal, chances are some of our children will turn out like one. I have to agree that pregnancy and motherhood does kill brain cells, but hey, give us some credit, right?

Some mothers are afraid of their doctors. They think that their doctor hates them calling or bringing their child in for every little thing. You are better safe than sorry. With kids, there are several times where you just can't tell whether there is a serious problem or not. I would rather be that annoying mother who has her child checked for everything than the mom who didn't take her child in for a checkup and is now very sorry for it. You know your child, and you need to do what your gut tells you to do. Don't feel bad if you feel like you are being a pest. This is what doctors get paid the big bucks for.

Middle Child Syndrome:

For those of you who have a middle child, never fear. As far as I'm concerned, middle child syndrome is not as bad as some studies make it out to be. However, I am not a middle child either. I recently read that middle children are typically less successful than their older and younger siblings and that they receive less financial help for college. Okay, what parent really pays for their older child's education, skips out on the middle child and then pays for the younger child's education? I guess I haven't ever seen that. You would think the oldest child would get less help because the parents still have two or more children at home to support.

Besides, if there is such a thing as middle child syndrome, then wouldn't middle children be the most motivated to make something of themselves just to "show" their parents and siblings? Most of the middle children I know are just as successful, if not more so, than their older and younger siblings. Unfortunately some parents do neglect their middle children. Hey, Suzy and Jimmy are going to get new shoes but Sarah won't because she's the middle child. If you are concerned about the middle child syndrome, then there is something you can do about it. Try to give all of your children special attention and try not to play favorites. You may wonder how a parent could possibly play favorites among their children, but it does happen.

I do know a mother who wanted four children so she wouldn't have a middle child. She was right, with four kids, you don't have a middle child; you have two of them!

Responsibility:

As with college, motherhood comes with a lot of responsibilities. We are in charge of another person's life and well-being. We aren't just in charge of making sure we aren't burning candles in our dorm rooms or getting our homework turned in on time. But just because we become a mother doesn't mean that we actually change a whole lot. I can still be pretty immature, as can a lot of other adults I know. I just don't do the same immature things I did in college.

My friend Becky and I aren't conducting fake psychology surveys anymore or convincing people that they are forced to share their room with the new foreign exchange student from Sweden who doesn't speak English and sleeps with a teddy bear. Once we put signs up saying that our friend Pete was giving guitar lessons and that the first ten callers got a free pick. Yeah, we were in trouble after Pete started receiving calls. He was a little upset and threatened to sneak into my dorm room at night and Nair off my eyebrows.

Now that I am several years older and a mother of two, I still have the same personality and am the same person. I called Becky up last year and told her that I couldn't make it to her wedding because I was in a car accident and my leg was broken. She died laughing when I told her I was just joking. We like to joke with each other like that.

I wouldn't go out and toilet paper someone's house or steal signs, but an occasional prank is still fun!

We also used to freak out people by telling them that we lived in the dorm room above them and that our large fish aquarium broke and that water would probably be leaking into their room any minute.

Messing with the answering machine was fun too. Our answering machine said something to the effect of ,"We are not in right now, please leave a message. But we can't guarantee we will call you back. I mean, what is a guarantee really, anyway? I could slap a guarantee on a box of cow pies and all you'd have is a guaranteed box of shit."

Now attending Mom U, my answering machine should say something to the effect of, "Thank you for calling the house of insanity. We are not responsible for the machine cutting you off in the middle of your message or making you wait on the line while it beeps ten million times. We will, however, return your call in the order in which it was received. Thank you."

Dealing with Your Kids:

At Mom U, I have designed a foolproof way of dealing with your kids. Stick your fingers in your ears, close your eyes and say "la, la, la" several times. Or I sing really loud so they think I am going nuts and then they start to laugh. Sometimes I talk in an accent or sing a song about them. I sing this song to the Wild Thing tune, "Codeman, you are a wild man. You making everything, groovy." Or I'll sing, "Montana, bana, bo bana, banana fana, fo fana, me, my, mo mana. Montana" Yes, it works to get their minds off what they were whining about.

Sometimes having kids makes you feel like one and you just want to skip, jump and eat at McDonald's a lot. I find myself treating them like younger siblings at times. It could be because I am a younger mother or because I miss picking on my little brother and sister who aren't so little anymore.

Kids can also be categorized in to several groups. You may have the quiet one, the rowdy one, the sleepless one, the loud one or the shy one. You may also have the bossy one, the smart one, the cute one, the athletic one, the picky one, the unique one or the mature one. You may also find that your child is a combination of several of these which just makes life that much more interesting.

Perfection:

Some of us want our kids to be perfect and some of us have the misconception that our kids really are perfect. Are we perfect? No, and that is what attracts people to us. Some of our little quirks are what people like best about us. It is our nature to want our children to be better than us in every way. We hope they are smarter, more athletic, better musicians, better looking, taller, shorter, thinner and more popular. Most parents don't get children with all of the attributes they hoped for. When it comes to our children, we need to remember that we are all made differently for a reason and that is why everyone is special in their own little ways. Really, how boring would this world be if everyone dressed the same, lived in identical homes, drove identical vehicles and fought for the same type of jobs? Life would be very dull, not to mention difficult.

Remember that we are all individuals when your child doesn't seem to be headed down the exact path that you had hoped for. We all have dreams for our children, but as parents, we must remember that those may not be the same dreams our children have for themselves. Our parents probably had big dreams for us too, and some of us lived up to our parents' expectations and others of us have not. When raising your children, try to remember those things your parents did to you that you swore you'd never do to your children because history has a funny way of repeating itself. If your parents pressured you to pursue sports but you wanted to be a cheerleader, don't pressure your child to become a cheerleader if they really want to pursue sports.

Sleep Deprivation:

At Mom U, you will experience some sort of sleep loss. It may be worse in the beginning, but throughout your education at Mom U, some sleep deprivation is normal at any stage of your education. I would get so tired when my kids were babies that I would put the milk in the cupboard or the dirty laundry in the garbage. I have even been walking around with my shirt on backwards and once found a pad on the outside of my underwear. I'm sure you all understand what is like to be exhausted. Now my kids are getting older, but we still have nights where they come into our room because they can't sleep. My daughter will bring in a pillow and blanket and sleep on our floor, but my son always tries to climb in bed with us. Then I get stuck between two people and am laying in that crack the two pillows make. I can't move and I start getting hot and then that's it, I won't fall asleep again. I usually try to wait until my son falls asleep and then move him back to his room. Sometimes this works, and sometimes the little pistol is back in our bed an hour later.

I have heard from mothers of teenagers that you lay awake waiting for them to come home at night. I remember always breaking curfew, and my parents would be so mad at me. Now that I'm a mother, I can imagine how they couldn't sleep until I got home.

Unlike in college, if you sleep past noon once you've become a mom, someone will check on you to make sure you are still alive. Sleeping past 8:00 a.m. rarely happens at Mom U.

How to Talk to a Mom U Student:

- Binky, Passy, Nook Nook – The plastic object with a rubber tip that infants like to suck on.
- Leaking – Milk being expressed from the breast at unexpected moments
- Fat – Squishy bulges that usually show up in the hips, thighs and mid-section
- Exhausted – Lack of sleep
- Multi-tasking – Being able to do ten things efficiently at the same time
- Telecommuter – Working from home for an outside business
- PMS – Pissed Mom Syndrome
- Flustered – Trying to take three kids to the grocery store and they find the racks of toys the store purposely puts near the checkout lines
- Annoyed – Trying to take care of the kids when you have the flu and your roommate is sacked out on the couch watching sports
- Devastated – When your child breaks the hand-painted china plate your great grandma gave you
- Irritated – when your roommate says, "I didn't like that plate anyway"
- Ticked-Off – When it gets back to you that a friend told your sister-in-law that your kids are "awful"
- Horny – I don't know what this word means anymore
- Delighted – When your son learns to aim at the pot
- Relieved – When your son actually hits the pot
- Ecstatic – When your husband watches the kids so you can go shopping with the girls
- Giddy – When someone tells you that you look much younger than you really are

- Diaper Bag – A purse
- Thongs – The only shoes that will fit in your ninth month of pregnancy
- Spit-Up – The white stuff your baby will spit on you right before you are ready to go somewhere
- Abnormal – Your husband's lack of hygiene skills
- Nut House – Your house
- Pumping – Hooking up a suction cup to your breasts to collect milk
- Exercising – Chasing the kids
- Emergency Room – The place where everybody knows your name
- Moo Moo – Maternity clothes
- Garage Sales – The sales you start shopping for all of your clothing and household needs
- Gas – What our kids have that they inherited from their father
- Music – Wooden spoons on pots, toy instruments and the flicking of that little springy door stopper behind the door
- Meals – Food you hope other people will invite you over for
- Stain Stick – The thing you hope you never run out of
- Baby – the one that cries
- Toddler – the one that destroys things
- Teen – the one with the attitude
- Bliss – a back massage
- Happiness – what your children have to offer you

Alcohol Policy:

Most mothers at Mom U are of legal age to drink and do enjoy a drink on occasion. We do hope that you drink wisely and always have a designated driver. Some of you may have become the designated driver due to your roommate's liking to alcohol.

Just a word to the wise, drinking activities that are potentially dangerous, such as "chugging" of alcoholic beverages, competitive drinking activities and activities that employ peer pressure to force participants to consume alcohol, are not safe. But neither is doing the above with milk, so you just have to use your best judgment. By judgment, I mean the decisions you would make when sober.

What Type of Grading Scale Does Mom U Have?

This is the best part about Mom U: there is no grading scale! Thank goodness we don't have to mess with this. Just do the best job you possibly can, love your child and you'll do just fine. Your roommate and his friends may grade you on a scale of one to ten, but that more than likely has nothing to do with being a mom.

Addictions:

Some students at Mom U develop addictions after having children. For instance, perhaps drinking pop, eating candy or having professional pictures taken of your new baby every month will become an addiction of yours. My addiction has become listening to country music. I would be glued to CMT if we had satellite, but we built a new house and decided not to get a dish. Yes, we have been satellite-free for over a year now. Most of you wonder how we do it; no Lifetime, no cartoons, and most of all, no sports for my husband. I'm about ready to break down and get satellite again just because my husband seems crabby dealing with his sports and hunting channel withdrawal.

I have a friend who has become addicted to chewing gum. She starts having chewing gum withdrawals if she doesn't get a piece. She's like a chain gum chewer.

Some women become addicted to buying scrap-booking supplies but never actually start a scrapbook. This is a strange disorder that needs to be addressed. If you know a mom like this, please invite her over for tea and scrap-booking. Or better yet, if she's not going to use the stuff, ask if you can borrow it!

Entertainment Opportunities:

There are so many fun things to do at Mom U. Besides the fun little things at home like playing on the swing set, building sand castles in the sandbox, riding bikes, renting movies and wrestling around, there are several outside of the home activities. Take the kids to a circus, amusement park, zoo, water park, swimming pool, roller skating rink, bowling alley, pizza place with a furry band and games, movie theater and the list goes on and on. When my siblings and I got older, my parents took us horseback riding, white-water rafting, camping in the mountains, Disney Land, Universal Studios, caves, wax museums and many more fun places.

There are also several extracurricular activities that are just for you and your roommate. Go to a movie, out for dinner, try bowling or roller-skating. I always thought it would be fun to go to a drive-in theater. I know there are only a few left in the state I live in. Whatever you do, it is important to have alone time with your roommate too! Some books I've read recommend having "date night" once a week. We try to go out once a month since hiring a baby sitter and going out can get rather costly.

SIDEBAR:

My son just asked me if he could watch a movie. He was wearing a shirt and his underwear inside out, sporting a nice skid mark on them. While I was getting him a clean pair of underwear, I noticed some liquid in a brand new beach bucket that was sitting in his room. When I asked him if he poured water or juice into the bucket he said, "No, I peed in it."

Section 23
Annual Events

Mother's Day is the main annual event at Mom U. We all celebrate this day in our own special ways. Some of us get homemade cards from the kids, candy, flowers, and diamonds. Whatever the gift, we love it. We know how great it feels to be remembered on Mother's Day, so don't ever forget your own mother or mother-in-law! These are a few Mother's Day cards that say it all about being a mother.

Mother's Day Cards:

From son:
Mom, since I've sucked you dry for the last 365 days, I decided that my sister should do the cleaning today. You can thank me later. Happy Mother's Day

From daughter:
I am sorry for being a brat and saying you look fat. I promise to keep my comments about your hair inside, and by your rules today, I will abide. With that, can I please borrow the car?

MOM UNIVERSITY

From husband:
Dana, or Danae, is it? I feel like I haven't seen you much this year, but thought I'd bring you some Mother's Day cheer. Enjoy the membership to the gym. I would've bought myself one but I am growing attached to my pudgy belly.

From a mother to her mother:
Mom, finally now I understand why you started gaining weight and going gray. I am joining the club.

From a child:
Mom, I love you, you are the best. Can we go to the park now? You promised.

From son:
Mom, you are more than a mom, you are my friend and friendship is like pissing your pants. You can feel its warmth and you always know it's there. Mom, you are the piss in my pants.

From daughter:
Dear Mom, remember the days when I used to sneak out of the house, steal the car and then drive around egging the teachers' houses with my friends? Wait, you did know about that, right? Well have a Happy Mother's Day.

From husband:
You are the best mom in the world. But please don't tell my mom I said that. I don't need her mad at me. I don't care what you tell your mother. Happy Mother's Day.

From son:
Mom, ykoju alrae ciodosl. Hsatvse a Hlaiphpey Mwobtshiemrys Deapy. (Some kids come up with the silliest cards)

From daughter:
When I have kids, if I start to sound like my mother, please slap me. Oh, wait, you are my mother. Ha, never mind. Happy Mother's Day.

From friend without kids:
You are one of the bravest women I have ever met. Keep up the good work; once they get to college, you'll have somewhat of a break. I didn't mean breakdown, because that just wouldn't happen to you, but a recess from the kids is more like it.

Section 24
Remember, We Forget

If there is one thing to be learned from this book it is this: a lot can be learned from a child. Even though we were children at one time, we do easily forget what it was like back then. Looking at our own children, it is hard to imagine that at one time we were their age. It just doesn't seem possible and we tend to forget so much.

We forget what it's like to swing on the swings, to dance in the rain and to roll in the grass. We forget what it is like to have no fear, to not care what others think and to be pure of heart. We forget what it was like to not know failure, not know rejection and not know cruelty. There was a time where we didn't see color, religion didn't matter and we were friends with everyone we knew. We forget what it was like to be carefree, to not know responsibility and to love others as they are.

Now that we are mothers, we can once again live in some ways like a child. Our children love us no matter our color, religion, appearance or income. We are mothers and to our children we are everything.

Go dance in the rain, swing on the swings, play kickball, roll in the grass, laugh and have fun. These are the gifts our children will give us. Someday they will grow up and someday they will forget. For now, they live life thinking we make the world go round. As mothers, we are all truly blessed.

I hope that Mom University is all that you dreamed it to be and much more. We are living longer and our children are only home for such a short time, so enjoy them now! Tell them you love them every day and be proud to be a mother. You can do the impossible!